THE ANATOMY OF

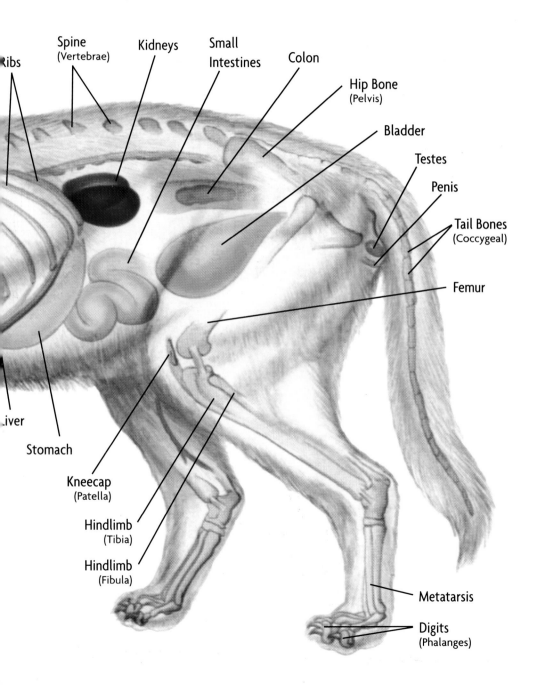

Ribs

Spine
(Vertebrae)

Kidneys

Small
Intestines

Colon

Hip Bone
(Pelvis)

Bladder

Testes

Penis

Tail Bones
(Coccygeal)

Femur

Liver

Stomach

Kneecap
(Patella)

Hindlimb
(Tibia)

Hindlimb
(Fibula)

Metatarsis

Digits
(Phalanges)

Devon Rex Cat

◇

By Chelsea King

CONTENTS

PUBLISHED IN THE UNITED KINGDOM BY:

INTERPET
PUBLISHING

Vincent Lane, Dorking   Surrey RH4 3YX   England

ISBN 1-84286-048-8

Photographs by Isabelle Francais and Alan Robinson with additional photographs by Michael W Brim, Cat Fanciers Association, Carolina Biological Supply, Fleabusters Rx for Fleas, James R Hayden, RBP, Interpet, Dwight R Kuhn, Dr Dennis Kunkel, Pet Profiles, Phototake, Jean Claude Revy and WB Saunders Company.

The publisher wishes to thank Shirley Oberheide, Paul and Dolores Spivack and all the owners of the cats in this book.

History of the

DEVON REX CAT

It can be said, with little fear of contradiction, that the Devon Rex is not the average person's concept of a typical feline. Looking something like a cross between a pixie and a cat from another world, this is very much a breed that will only appeal to those whose tastes are unusual, yet do not quite stretch to outrageous.

With an impish-like face, the Devon Rex enjoys a strong following of devotees who find it not only a beautiful cat to behold but also one which overflows with a delightful charm and cheekiness that make it a wonderful companion. The Devon has the distinction of being one of only three anatomically-based mutational breeds presently recognised by the Governing Council of the Cat Fancy (GCCF) in Britain, the Cornish Rex and the Manx being the other two.

The charm and uniqueness of the Devon Rex are such that it now enjoys status with every major cat registry in the world. It is always the source of great interest when seen by cat lovers for the first time, and certainly ranks as one of those breeds that 'grow' on you the more you become familiar with it.

MUTATIONAL BREEDS

A mutational breed is one that has been developed from a spontaneous mutation. These natural happenings occur in all animal species and are normally very minor and imperceptible. They are the vehicles of evolution by which animals develop from one species into another. But occasionally a mutation will be of a major type that is very obvious.

In the wild, mutations are Nature's attempts to achieve quantum leap evolution. Only very rarely do they prove of benefit to a species, so they fail to survive. However, under domestic conditions they can be retained. Many domestic animal breeds are based on mutations, and these include a number of cat breeds. In most of these, only one feature of the cat's anatomy is altered, such as the ear shape, tail length or fur type. But in the Devon Rex, the mutation has a double effect.

The basis of the mutation is that it alters the cat's fur type. However, in the process, it also changes the individual's genetic background for its body anatomy, especially that of the head, which is very unique to this breed. Before discussing the history and other aspects of this most unusual feline, it is beneficial for the newcomer to understand how the rex coat differs from that of normal cats.

THE TERM *REX*

The term *rex* (meaning royal), as applied to cats, is named after the Castor Rex rabbit, which was developed as an exhibition breed in France during 1919. Its fur was shorter than normal and its coat colour pattern was similar to that of the beaver, whose scientific name is *Castor fiber*. Subsequently, the name 'rex' was used in other small pets, such as mice, hamsters, guinea pigs and cats to denote a hair type. The name 'Castor' is still used in rabbits to denote the brown colour.

Since the rex coat was first identified, numerous other types have appeared, which differ significantly to that in the rabbit.

They have been given appropriate names that indicate their type of rex. Two such examples are the fuzzy and the astrex. The fur of the Devon Rex is more comparable to the fuzzy rex of the mouse than that displayed by the various rex rabbit breeds.

THE REX COAT

A cat's coat is created by three hair types that are called guard, awn (bristle) and down. The guard hairs are the longest and coarsest in their texture. The awn hairs, also called the secondary guard hairs, are shorter and thinner, while the down hairs are the shortest, thinnest and softest of the hair types.

Each of the types has a characteristic shape, with the guard hairs being smooth while the down hairs are crimped along their length. The awn hairs display a midway shape between

The three types of hair—guard, awn and down— are present in the Devon Rex, yet each type is thinner and shorter than in normally-coated cats, resulting in an overall sparser coat.

A Devon Rex coloured like a chocolate Siamese, sometimes called a Si-Rex.

the other two. They are such that at the extremes of their natural range of variation they might be mistaken for guard or down hairs.

The function of the outer or topcoat (guard and awn hairs) is to create excellent protection against inclement weather. The soft down hair (undercoat or underfur) provides insulation that minimises bodily heat loss. This requires the protection of the topcoat to be fully effective. The coat may be compared with a person wearing a raincoat over a woollen jumper.

In the fur of the Devon Rex, the guard hairs become shorter, thinner and sparser. They also take on a soft, wavy appearance. The awn hairs also become shorter, thinner and wavy. They are hardly distinguishable from the down hairs, which also become shorter. The whiskers (vibrissae) of this breed become very brittle, tending to break. This results in either missing whiskers

or those that are little more than stubble of various lengths.

The fur is at its shortest on the neck. There is a quite wide potential for the quality of the coat. This means that in some

THE CRYSTAL PALACE SHOW

On 13 July 1871, an event took place that changed the world of the domestic cat. In the Crystal Palace at Sydenham, London, the world's first all-breed cat show took place. It was organised by Harrison Weir (1824–1906), a noted animal artist and great lover of cats.

The success of the cat show saw Weir become a noted cat judge and author. Today he is regarded as the 'father of the cat fancy.'

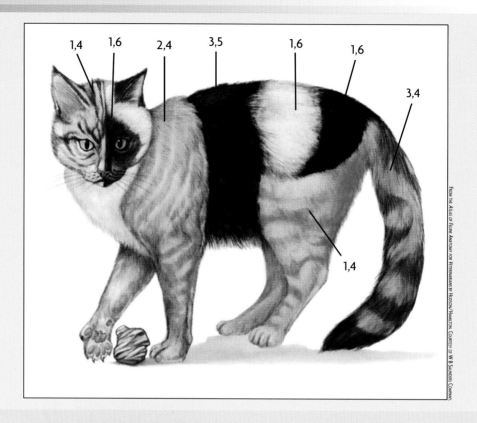

1,4 1,6 2,4 3,5 1,6 1,6 3,4 1,4

FROM THE *ATLAS OF FELINE ANATOMY FOR VETERINARIANS* BY HUDSON/HAMILTON. COURTESY OF W B SAUNDERS COMPANY.

PARTICOLOURED CAT

Not a new breed of feline, this 'particoloured cat' illustrates the many possibilities of the feline coat. Since cats come in three basic hair lengths, short, long and rex (curly), all three coat lengths are illustrated here. Additionally, different coat patterns, such as mackerel tabby, Abyssinian and self-coloured, are depicted to demonstrate the differences.

1–3 COAT TYPES
  1 Shorthair coat
  2 Rex (curly) coat
  3 Longhair coat

4–6 COAT COLOUR PATTERNS
  4 Mackerel (tabby)
  5 Abyssinian
  6 Self-coloured

SKIN AND HAIRCOAT OF CATS

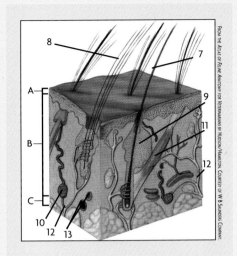

Schematic illustration of histologic layers of the integument skin.

A Epidermis
B Dermis
C Subcutis

7 Primary hair
8 Secondary hairs
9 Area of sebaceous gland
10 Apocrine sweat gland
11 M arrector pili
12 Nerve fibre
13 Cutaneous vessels
14 Tactile hair
15 Fibrous capsule
16 Venous sinus
17 Sensory nerve fibres
18 External root sheath
19 Hair papilla

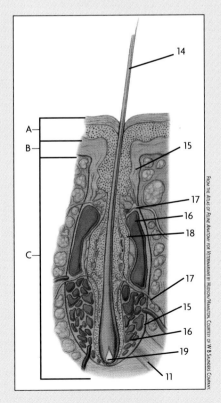

Schematic illustration of a tactile hair (whisker).

FROM THE ATLAS OF FELINE ANATOMY FOR VETERINARIANS BY HUDSON/HAMILTON. COURTESY OF W B SAUNDERS COMPANY

FROM THE ATLAS OF FELINE ANATOMY FOR VETERINARIANS BY HUDSON/HAMILTON. COURTESY OF W B SAUNDERS COMPANY

The Cornish Rex derives from a different mutation than its cousin, the Devon Rex, and has been longer established than the Devon breed.

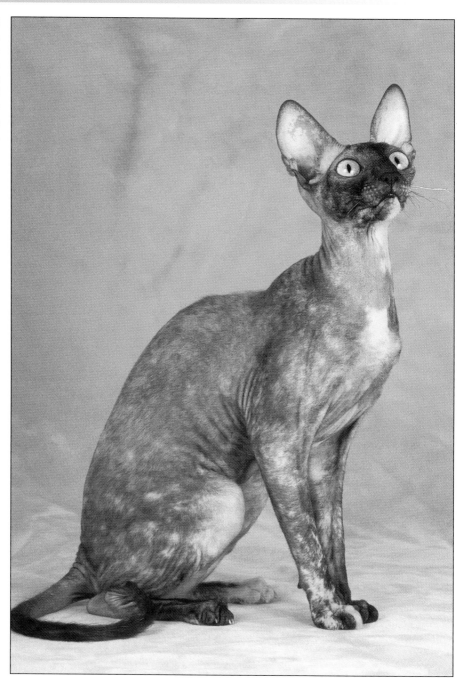

individuals the extent of sparsely furred areas is greater than in others. Kittens should therefore be selected with care to ensure, as far as is possible, they have been bred from superior-coated stock.

THE FIRST REX BREEDS

Rex cats have appeared many times over the years in various countries, but the first of these to be fully developed was the Cornish Rex. A German Rex, though appearing earlier than the Cornish mutation, was not fully developed to breed status. It was eventually absorbed into the Cornish breed, though use of its name has been revived in some European countries.

The Cornish Rex was first seen during 1950 in an old farmhouse on Bodmin Moor in the county after which it was eventually to be named. It was initially called the English Rex (also Poodle Rex, or Astrex for its similarity to Astrakhan sheepskin).

Ten years later, in 1960, in the adjoining county of Devon, a male rex cat was seen living around a disused tin mine near the delightful village of Buckfastleigh on the edge of Devon's famous Dartmoor. This male rex is believed to have been the sire of the cat that was to become the father of the second rex breed to be developed.

THE BIRTH OF A BREED

Attempts to capture the feral rex male proved futile, but fate was to play its hand and consequently

THE BREED IN AMERICA

In 1968, Alison Ashford was the first person to export breeding stock of the Devon to America in the form of Annelida Sunset Cream. The importers were Marion White and her daughter Anita who lived in Austin, Texas. Although it had already been established in Britain that the Devon and Cornish Rex mutations were quite different, thus the basis of separate breeds, this fact was not initially appreciated by all American registries.

The first association to grant the Devon status was the American Cat Fanciers Association (ACFA) in 1972. The Cat Fanciers Association (CFA) chose to lump the two rexes together, and the Devon was judged against a standard that was essentially written based on a mix of the Cornish and German Rex types. The situation was totally unacceptable because it was unworkable from a practical breeding viewpoint.

Fortunately, logic eventually prevailed and the CFA granted the Devon its separate breed status in 1979, at which time the Devon Rex Breed Club came into being. The Devon gained championship status in 1983. However, it remained very much a rare breed, and as late as 1989 its breed club had only a handful of members. But as the breed gained more promotion via exhibition and media exposure, and as its coat quality improved, the number of annual registrations steadily started to climb.

give rise to the Devon Rex. Miss Beryl Cox, the lady who had been observing the elusive male, was acquainted with a tortie and white female stray that roamed the same area. She was a normal-coated cat of typical domestic type.

In due course, she gave birth to a litter in a field that adjoined the garden of Miss Cox. On inspecting the litter, Beryl was delighted to see a male curly-coated kitten. She took the kitten (some accounts say the litter) and reared it in her home. Its colour was a dusky dark grey-black, being darkest on the face, legs and tail. Beryl gave the male the name of Kirlee.

At this point, a general genetic comment needs to be made. In order to produce a rex kitten, Kirlee's mother must have been carrying the rex gene in single dose. If it is assumed she obtained this from the elusive Dartmoor male, then Kirlee's father and grandfather was the same cat.

However, this roaming male no doubt enjoyed more than a few romantic interludes in his travels. This meant that all of his apparently normal offspring would be carrying the rex gene. Any of his male offspring could, therefore, have been the sire of Kirlee.

KIRLEE GOES TO STUD
Beryl Cox was aware of the English Rex, which had gained

ADVANTAGES AND DISADVANTAGES
The obvious negative aspect of any rex coat is that it does not provide, in comparison with the normal coat, protection against extremes of weather, be this hot, cold or wet. It is a breed that requires more consideration of this fact if it is to be given outdoor freedom to exercise during the extremes of weather conditions.

Clearly, it is well suited to indoor-only living. Additionally, it does not shed as much fur as does the normal feline. For those who suffer from allergies, in particular those related to cat fur, the coat of the Devon minimises (but does not prevent) the risk of allergies and their severity. Consequently, many people who might not have been able to own a cat have enjoyed the true companionship of a feline. They have found the coat of the Devon Rex does not prompt any negative reaction in them. The fur of the Devon is shed in the normal manner, but as there is less of it, and it is shorter than normal, it is far less obvious than with cats having typical feline fur.

Grooming the Devon is a breeze; indeed, excessive grooming would be detrimental to the coat. This is because some of the more loosely rooted guard hairs could more easily be groomed out of the fur than would be the case with a normal feline coat.

The Devon Rex coat is easy to care for and sheds less than that of any other normally coated cat. The coat is thin and does not provide much protection against extremes in the weather.

DEVELOPING THE BREED

In order to develop the Devon it was necessary to both inbreed to Kirlee and his offspring, as well as to outcross to other breeds.

Inbreeding is required whenever there is only a small genetic pool to work with. This is invariably the case with new breeds. It also rapidly fixes in desired aspects of the breed's anatomy, but it also fixes in any undesirable genes as well.

The outcross is essential to introduce hybrid vigour, thus counterbalancing the negatives of excessive inbreeding, and to introduce any new colours or patterns that are felt would be beneficial to the breed's future. It also helps to rapidly widen the gene pool. A purebred outcross is always the preferred choice because the breeder is more aware of the features that will be present in the hybrid offspring.

When moggie (mongrel) types are used, these may be carrying all sorts of unwanted recessive (thus hidden) genes in their genetic make-up. The inter-breeding of any of the differing rex breeds is not recommended, as this offers no benefit to those rex mutations that have been developed into specific breeds.

much local and national media attention. She assumed that Kirlee was of the same genotype and that he would be a useful cat to have in the breeding programme of this unusual developing breed. Not coming from the same immediate area, she felt he would help widen the gene pool.

Miss Cox eventually contacted Brian Sterling-Webb, a well-known figure in the cat hobby. He had been involved in the development of the Cornish Rex, as well as the Colourpoint Persian, where his genetic knowledge was put to good use. He persuaded Miss Cox to let him have Kirlee so he could be mated with various Cornish Rex queens. The matings were duly effected and all concerned were naturally very excited to see the kittens from this new stud.

DISAPPOINTMENT

It must have been quite a blow when not one single kitten was born with a rex coat. Kirlee was then mated to other rex queens and carriers but, alas, the results were the same. However, when normal-coated offspring of the English Rex x Kirlee cats were mated to each other, some rex kittens were produced. This clearly indicated that separate mutations were involved, and that the Kirlee rex was inherited in the same recessive manner as that of the English Rex.

Yet it was impossible to say

An odd-eyed tortie tabby Devon Rex, representing the modern incarnation of the breed.

which type the offspring were— the English or the Kirlee mutation—until further matings were effected. This is because such a mating had the theoretical potential to produce both types, as well as normal-coated kittens that were carrying both the English and Kirlee mutations.

It must be remembered that the striking difference between the bodily appearance of the two types today was not as obvious in the 1960s. The influence of the Cornish body type on that of the Devon resulted in individuals that could have been mistaken for either rex type.

As Kirlee was not of the English Rex genotype, it was obvious that a totally fresh breeding programme would be needed to establish a breeding pool based on his variety of the rex. The English Rex was therefore designated rex mutant 1 and given the genetic symbol of r, while the Kirlee variety became mutant 2 with the symbol of re. At this point, the English Rex was named the Cornish Rex while the Kirlee type became the Devon Rex.

BREEDING SUCCESS

With an understanding of the genotypes, it became possible to reproduce Kirlee's type without problem. He was mated to numerous breeds, which included the British Shorthair, Siamese, Russian Blue, Burmese and others.

As expected, no rex kittens were born. But all the kittens were carrying the Devon rex mutation. These offspring were then mated back to Kirlee and—*voila!*—rex kittens were produced. The theoretical expectations from such matings are that 50% of the offspring will be homozygous (pure-breeding) Devon Rex, with 50% being heterozygous (non-pure-breeding) normal-coated kittens, but carrying the Devon Rex gene.

GAINING RECOGNITION

Being unusual types, both of the now separate rex breeds developed slowly because breeders were not actually queuing up to obtain them. It was said that even after nine years from its first appearance, there were less that one hundred Devon Rex in the world, but this figure was probably on the low side. The types also had their critics who felt they were undesirable 'sports' better left alone than developed. The Devon, with it very unusual facial features, coupled with baldness problems, certainly was regarded as somewhat of a freak in its early days.

Another problem was that noted judges and authors of the day were on record as stating the type could never be given breed status. In the 1961 edition of *The Observer's Book of Cats*, Grace Pond stated 'that "rex" is not a new breed of cat.' She continued to point out that, as it was purely a coat type, 'no new breed number would be necessary.' Others regarded the breed as a novelty that would vanish as had so many others over the years.

But thanks to the diligence of their most devoted enthusiasts, both rexes eventually gained official recognition. The basis of breed definition changed with the passage of years (and continues to do so), and the arrival of the Devon Rex certainly indicated it wasn't just a coat type that was involved, but rather a breed in the making on the basis of its appearance as well. The early coat problems in the breed were largely eradicated by selective breeding from only the best-coated individuals.

In 1967 the two rexes were given separate recognition and championship status. The Devon standard was drafted on Kirlee's body type and the breed number allocated to it was 33a (33 being the Cornish Rex). To complete the history of the early years of this delightful breed, it has to be stated that Kirlee, the breed's father, lived a happy life with friends of Brian Sterling-Webb until 1970. Kirlee was then involved in a road

accident, which sadly proved fatal to him.

FUTURE OF THE BREED

Although the Devon looks the sort of breed that could easily have become a fad or fashion breed, this never in fact has happened. The singular advantage of this is that it has changed little since its formative years and has retained a very stable nucleus of dedicated breeders.

There is little doubt that in future years the Devon is destined to become progressively more popular on a global basis. Its numbers increase each year in Great Britain and mainland European countries, as they do in Australia and other countries far removed from the land of its origin. Its combination of unusual looks and kitten-like behaviour patterns will continue to beguile all those who come into contact with it.

A white Devon Rex, exhibiting blue eye coloration.

Giant ears and prominent round eyes give the Devon Rex a pixie-like image.

A Portrait of the

DEVON REX CAT

One thing that is certain in respect to the Devon Rex is that once it is seen, it is never forgotten. This is one of those breeds that really is very different from all others. With its huge ears and prominent round eyes, it really does have a pixie look about it. The Devon is a relatively small breed and females average about 2.7 kgs (6 lbs), males being rather heavier at about 3.4 kgs (7.5 lbs). However, the breed feels heavier than it looks due to its hard muscle.

OFFICIAL BREED DESCRIPTION

The official description of any breed is its breed standard. This is normally drafted by its national breed club and presented to one of the national registries for adoption by them. The standard then becomes the yardstick by which all cats of that breed are assessed by show judges and breeders.

The standard is based on a theoretically ideal individual. As such, it is open to interpretation by judges and breeders. In many ways it is a somewhat vague document because of the very fact that it can never be precise. All standards use many relative terms and these can be rather difficult for the newcomer to understand.

For example, terms such as moderate length, medium size and strong chin only have meaning if a person actually views many outstanding examples of the breed. Once a mental image of what the relative terms mean has been acquired, the standard becomes a more useful document. It is then possible to make judgements on which are poor specimens.

The only way a breed enthusiast can develop the needed appreciation of the standard is by visiting many cat shows at which top breed winners are present. Discussing the finer points with leading breeders and show judges then completes the novice's education of the Devon breed standard.

There are many feline registries around the world today, most operating within a single nation. But some have now expanded and are international in their sphere of influence. Each registry has its own breed standards, and these are rarely exact duplicates of others, yet they are very similar in essence.

The following breed description is not that of any single

registry, but is based on comparing a number of these. Comments are included where appropriate to clarify some technical terms. The description should meet the needs of most owners. Hobbyists planning to breed or exhibit their Devon Rex should obtain the standard(s) of the registry(s) with which their cats are registered.

HEAD
Viewed from the front, the head has the appearance of a modified wedge in which curves are seen on the outer edges of the ears, on the cheekbones and on the whisker pads. The muzzle is short, displaying a strong chin and whisker break (the area

The head of the Devon Rex, when viewed from the front, appears as a modified wedge. The nose is well defined and the eyes are large and oval.

behind the whisker pad).

The nose is well defined. It creates a definite stop (change of angles) where it meets the forehead, which gently curves to the flat skull. The cheekbones are well pronounced.

EYES
The eyes are large, oval, set wide and a prominent facial feature. They display a slight angle towards the nose.

EYE COLOUR
Any eye colour is acceptable, though the body colour or pattern will normally dictate the colour. For example, in colour-point individuals, the colour will be blue, which is typical for this pattern. In white cats, the colour will be either blue, yellow-orange or odd-eyed, meaning one blue and one orange. Copper, amber, green and aquamarine are other common colours.

EARS
Possibly the most striking feature of this breed is the size of its ears, which, in relation to head size, are proportionately larger than in any other cat breed. They are set low and wide apart, and exhibit a very wide base. The curved outer edge of the ears extends beyond the lines of the facial wedge. The tips of the ears are rounded and may sport small tufts of hair.

BODY

Slender and of medium length, the body should be of hard musculature. The chest is broad and carried high on the legs, while the neck is slim and of medium length.

LEGS

The legs are slender and of good length. The hind legs are longer than those of the front, more so than in most other cat breeds.

PAWS

The paws should be small and oval. The front paws have five claws (one being the dewclaw), while the hind paws have four.

TAIL

The tail should be long, fine and tapering. It should be well covered with short fur.

COAT

Very short and of fine texture, the coat is wavy and curly, often having the appearance of being gently rippled. It is most dense on the body, legs, tail, face and ears, being less dense on the skull, neck, chest and abdomen. The presence of short guard hairs is acceptable. Whiskers and eyebrows are crinkled, somewhat coarse and medium in length.

BREED FAULTS

In cats, there are two main categories of faults. There are those that are applicable to all cat breeds, the other being those specific to the individual breeds. Here we are concerned only with breed-specific faults. In some instances, faults may result only in loss of points; in others, they may result in the withholding of

The coat of the Dexon Rex is very short and fine, most dense on the body, legs, tail, face and ears. This is a chocolate.

major awards. The most serious faults would result in disqualification of the exhibit. In some registries, all-breed faults are included within the breed faults, while in other registries they are not.

MAJOR FAULTS
Straight or shaggy coat, bare patches of fur in adults (not to be confused with down-only fur on the underparts), long, narrow or rounded head, straight profile (meaning lack of

This chocolate tortie illustrates the breed's large ears, the Devon Rex's most striking feature. The ears curve on the outer edge and are desirably large for the size of the head.

stop), small or high-set ears, kink in the tail, incorrect number of toes, crossed eyes (called a squint in Britain), weak hind legs and incorrect alignment of the teeth (overshot or undershot).

FAULTS
Cobby type body, lack of firm muscle, bare patches in kittens (not to be confused with down-only fur on the underparts) and short, bare or bushy tail.

DEVON REX SELF-COLOURS

COLOUR	DESCRIPTION
White	This should be a pure white, free of coloured hairs, though a few on the head of a kitten are not penalised. White in cats is created by a dominant mutation that is epistatic to all other colours (it masks their presence). The colour is linked to uni- or bilateral deafness, which is more likely in blue-eyed cats than in those with yellow eyes. Statistics suggest that about 45% of white cats are affected. Whites may be odd-eyed, meaning that they have one blue and one yellow.
Black	This is a dense lustrous black, free of rusty tinges, which may be genetic or due to excessive exposure to sunlight. This colour is called ebony in some breeds of American associations.
Seal	Seal is the term used for the very dark brown seen in the colourpointed pattern. It is a degradation of black linked to the colour restriction gene that creates the Siamese, Tonkinese and Burmese breeds.
Blue	In cats, blue is better described as a slate blue or grey. It is created by the effect on black of what is called the dilution gene. This does not actually dilute black, but clumps the pigment within the cells, thus its density changes. The resulting non-pigment areas create the illusion of dilution.
Chocolate	This is a medium to dark brown created by a mutation that degrades black. It is known as champagne in a number of American registries.
Lilac	A warm dove grey, lilac is created by the dilution of chocolate. It is alternatively called platinum, lavender or frost grey in some American registries.
Cinnamon	This is a lighter, more reddish shade of chocolate created by a second mutation at the black locus.
Fawn	Pale pinkish mushroom or rose beige, fawn is the dilution of cinnamon.
Caramel	This is a pale blue-fawn. It is one of the latest colours to be seen in cats and is created by a dominant gene called the dilute modifier that affects the way the dilution gene works. It, therefore, only alters the colour of the blue, lilac and fawn, which become caramel, and the cream, which becomes apricot.
Red	Ideally, this is a deep and rich brick red rather than the paler ginger orange seen in typical moggie cats. This is the only sex-linked colour known in cats and is responsible for the tortoiseshell pattern.
Cream	A pale to medium cream, this colour can also be described as buff. It is created by the dilution of red.
Apricot	This is an intense pinkish cream. The dilution modifier gene working on cream creates it.

HEREDITARY MYOPATHY

There is one major problem that is at this time of concern to serious Devon Rex breeders. Potential owners, and especially breeders, should be aware of the problem so they can research more information before purchasing breeding stock.

The condition is known as hereditary myopathy, which is often, and erroneously, called spasticity. It results in individuals not being able to hold their heads up correctly, having weakness in their walking patterns and sometimes other minor muscle problems. However, the condition appears not to be progressive, meaning it is limited and does not spread throughout the body once the condition has reached a certain stage.

The problem appears to be caused by a recessive gene, though geneticists are not sure if more than one gene is involved. At this time much research is being devoted to the condition, which, it must be added, can appear in any cat breed. Clearly, potential breeders should join their national breed club and be as informed as possible about the problem.

Pedigree research should be done before obtaining breeding stock. It should be stressed that the incidence of the problem is low, and the best way to ensure it remains that way, and hopefully is eliminated, altogether, is by awareness of its existence.

COLOURS AND PATTERNS

The Devon Rex is one of the small number of breeds that is accepted in any recognised colour or pattern, which includes any white markings on any coat pattern. This means the theoretical number of combinations from which an owner can choose is over one thousand. But, in real terms, the number is such that many combinations will range from difficult to locate to virtually non-existent. Choice will normally be restricted to the more popular colours and patterns.

No association includes descriptions of all possible combinations as part of the Devon Rex standard, though the CFA is one that does list a number of these. For the person wishing for more detail, refer to the Official Standard of Points booklet from your registry association. In this will be found the standards for all breeds. All of the colours and patterns of these are acceptable in the Devon Rex. Alternatively, cat-specific genetic books will also describe and discuss all presently available colours and patterns.

SELF-COLOURS

When a cat has the same colour all over its body, it is called a self-colour. It should be free of white or any other coloured hairs and be the same shade over the entire coat, down to the hair's root. However, some shading is often seen, generally by the colour's becoming paler on the underparts.

All self-colours display a range of shades and this can result in certain of them, in particular those based on brown, being mistaken for others. In cats, a colour that is created by a particular mutation may be given different names in different breeds, and/or different registry associations.

The self-colours are white, seal, black, blue, chocolate, lilac, cinnamon, fawn, caramel, red, cream and apricot. As a general guide, the colour of the nose leather and paw pads will match the colour of the coat, or be pink if the coat is of a very light colour.

Coat Patterns

A coat pattern is created when two or more colours combine in a definite manner. Likewise, two patterns can combine to create a more composite pattern. When the many colours are combined with the numerous patterns, this creates the extensive array of colour combinations possible in domestic cats.

Tabby: This pattern is available in four varieties: mackerel, classic or blotched, spotted and ticked. The basic common feature in each variety is the 'M' mark seen on the

COAT PATTERNS

Agouti	Pigments band the hair, named after the rodent that possesses this pattern.
Non-agouti	Coat colour exhibits a self-colour or carries two or more colours.
Shell	Darker colour on tips of the hair; lower portion lighter in colour.
Shaded	Darker colour extends further than the tip, as in the shell.
Bicolour	Solid colour with white pattern.

forehead, together with various stripes that extend from the eyes, and others that pass over the skull to the neck. The legs and tail are variously banded with complete or incomplete rings. The ground colour is an agouti mix of yellow and brown with black tipping on which a solid colour is superimposed.

Colourpoint: This is the name given to the Siamese pattern when it is seen in other breeds. The face, ears, legs and tail are a darker colour than the rest of the body, while the eyes are brilliant blue. The pattern can be combined with the tabby and or tortoiseshell patterns. Genetically it is known as the Siamese colour restriction.

Burmese: Imagine a colourpoint pattern, with the body colour almost as dark as the points. You now have the Burmese pattern, genetically called the Burmese colour restriction. It is the darkest of a series of mutations that go from full colour through Burmese, Tonkinese, Siamese, and blue-eyed white to albino.

The blue-eyed white of this series is rare and should not be confused with the blue-eyed dominant white. When the Siamese and Burmese patterns are combined, they create a pattern mid-way between the two. This is called Tonkinese and is an obligate hybrid.

Bicolour: In this pattern, a colour or pattern is combined with white. The placement and extent of the white are not important in the Devon Rex, but ideally one-third, and not more

VARIETIES OF TABBY PATTERNS

COLOUR	DESCRIPTION
Mackerel Tabby	The characteristic features are horizontal stripes that are seen on the sides of the body. The more of these there are, the better. This pattern variety is that of the wild ancestors of the domestic cat. It is commonly called 'tiger' in America.
Classic or Blotched Tabby	A large, oyster-like blotch on each flank that is surrounded by unbroken swirls is the identifying feature of this very popular and striking pattern.
Spotted Tabby	In this variety, the body is covered with various oval, round or rosette-shaped spots. These should be randomly placed on the body and not appear like the broken lines of the mackerel pattern.
Ticked Tabby	This pattern is genetically called agouti after the South American rodent. It comprises hairs that are banded in light and dark colours along their length. The lie of the coat then allows the dark parts of the hair shafts to be seen, thus creating the ticked effect originally made famous in the Abyssinian breed.

Chocolate tortie.

than one-half, should be white. Some of this is preferred to be on the head, ears, cheeks, back, tail, legs and flanks. Flexibility in the extent and placement is because the pattern is created by the presence of the white spotting gene, which is random in its effect.

Mi-Ke: Pronounced *mee-kay*, this pattern is basically a tricolour in which a white coat is blotched with red and black. It is one of a number of varieties seen in the Japanese Bobtail, from which it is taken.

Chocolate.

Si-Rex chocolate.

Brown.

Si-Rex chocolate.

Tipped Patterns: This is when part of the hair is tipped with colour pigment while the lower portion is as near to white as possible. There are three types of tipping. In the smoke, the top two-thirds of the hair is pigmented; in the shaded, only one-third is pigmented; while in the chinchilla, the pigment is restricted to the very tips of the hair. If the tipped patterns are of red colour, they are known as cameo.

Tortoiseshell: Commonly known as tortie, the pattern is a mix of red hairs, of various shades, and black. Red is a sex-linked and is dominant in its mode of transmission. Its effect is to replace black pigment with red.

The gene works in the following manner. A male's sex chromosomes comprise one designated as X and one that is Y.

White kitten.

White.

Black.

Black smoke.

Brown tabby kitten.

the dominant O is not able to mask it, as would normally be the case.

The coat is therefore covered with some areas that are red, while others are covered with any colour other than red. If the dilution gene is present, the red will become cream, while black will become blue to create the blue-cream.

The tortie pattern is thus seen only in females, unless a gene

The female has two X-chromosomes. The X chromosome can carry colour but the shorter Y does not and appears to be essentially concerned with gender-related traits. The colour red is designated as O for orange.

A male is either XO, a red cat; or Xo, a non-red (meaning any other colour). The female can be XOXO, a red cat; XoXo, a non-red cat; or XOXo, a tortoiseshell. The uniqueness of this pattern lies in the fact that the o of the XOXo, although a recessive and in a single dose, is able to visually express itself in the coat because

a colour or pattern (tabby or
tortie) is seen on the head, tail
and legs, but not on the body
(though one or two small patches
are acceptable).

Mitted: This pretty pattern is
best described as a colourpoint
pattern, but with the lower legs'
being white. It is the pattern of
the Birman and Ragdoll breeds.

Chocolate tortie.

Odd-eyed Tortie
Tabby.

abnormality is present in a male,
usually sterile. Such males have
appeared in the Devon Rex.
Combined with white, the tortie
creates the attractive tortie and
white pattern also called tricolour
or particolour. In America it is
called calico. Combined with the
tabby pattern, it is called the
torbie.

Van: This pattern is named
after the Turkish Van breed. It is
essentially a white coat on which

Purchasing a
DEVON REX CAT

Before the decision to purchase a Devon Rex is made, careful consideration should be given to the implications and responsibilities of cat ownership. If more owners would do this, there would be far fewer half-starved pets roaming our streets or living in local animal-rescue centres.

OWNER RESPONSIBILITY
The initial cost of a Devon Rex represents only a fraction of its lifetime's cost. The first question is, 'Can you afford one?' The kitten needs vaccinations to protect it against various diseases. Boosters are then required every year. Cat food is more costly than that for dogs. There is also the cost of cat litter every week. Periodic vet checks and treatment for illness or accident must be allowed for. When holidays are taken, you may need to board the pet at a cattery.

From the outset there will be additional costs apart from that of the kitten. It will need a basket, carrying box, feeding and grooming utensils, scratching post, a few toys and maybe a collar. If you have any doubts at all about being able to supply all

these needs, it is best not to obtain a cat.

Other matters also need careful thought. If you are planning to have a family, will your love for the Devon Rex be compromised once a baby arrives? Cats are generally not a problem with family newcomers providing they are not ignored or treated as being a threat to the baby. Never purchase a kitten for a child unless you want one yourself. If you are elderly, it is only fair to consider what would happen to your cherished pet if it were to outlive you or if you were to become hospitalised for long periods.

It is most unfortunate that many people rush into the purchase of cats on impulse. They then find they cannot cope if problems, and extra costs, ensue. Some lose interest in the pet once it matures past its kitten stage. The evidence of these realities is easily seen in the growing number of cats abandoned or taken to animal shelters every year. Invariably their owners will make feeble excuses for why the cat cannot be kept. But the bottom line is they did not stop to consider at the outset what responsible ownership entailed.

The Devon Rex is a very lively breed and therefore likely to get itself involved in everything that is happening in its immediate environment. It will develop very strong bonds of affection and dependency with its owner.

It will tend to do some things the average cat will not. These things will range from opening doors and cupboards, to being able to use press-type taps. None of these, including the breed's famed tail-wagging, is unique to the Devon. They, and other comparable behaviours, are seen in most breeds (though more so in those which are somewhat similar in stature to the Devon).

It is thus the complicated mix of conformation, temperament, intelligence and the genes it has inherited over many generations that all combine to create the full package of the breed. The environment and the nature of its owners are then the final dressing that will determine the patterns of behaviour. The Devon Rex is very much a breed best suited to the dedicated cat lover, who will bring out the very best from this amusing, cheerful, cheeky and very companionable little feline pixie.

KITTEN OR ADULT?

Most potential owners normally want a kitten because it is so cute,

THE PURCHASING PROCESS

Never rush into the purchase of a companion that is to be given the freedom of your home and will become an integral part of your life. A pure-bred cat may live 20 or more years. This is a long time. It is very prudent to take all those steps that will minimise the chances of your ever regretting the choice you make. Once you have decided on the sex, age, reason for purchase (pet, show or breeding) and desired colour pattern, proceed cautiously, heeding all the advice given here. By following a planned process of selection, you will also gain much useful information.

DOCUMENTATION

When you take delivery of your kitten, certain paperwork should come with it:

1. Three- to five-generation pedigree.
2. Breeder-signed registration application form or change of owner registration form. This assumes the breeder has registered stock. If they have not, the kitten cannot be registered at a later date. It is worth less than the kitten with registration paperwork. You are not recommended to purchase a kitten from unregistered parents.
3. Certificates of health, vaccination and neutering, if this has been effected. Ideally, it is desirable that the kitten's parents have been tested negative for major diseases. Additionally, the breeder should know the blood group of your kitten. This may be of importance at a later date.
4. Details of worming or other treatments attended.
5. Diet sheet, feeding timetable and brand names of food items used. This diet should be maintained for at least ten days while the kitten adjusts to the trauma of moving home.
6. Signed receipt for monies paid.
7. Signed copy of any guarantees. Not all breeders give a guarantee on the reasonable grounds that once the kitten leaves their care, its onward well-being is no longer under their control.

cuddly and playful. A kitten is easily trained and has not yet developed bad habits, which the older Devon Rex may have done. This said, if you plan to breed or exhibit, there are advantages in obtaining a young adult. Other potential owners, such as the elderly, may benefit by avoiding the demanding needs of a young kitten. In both these instances, a good age is when the youngster is 9 –15 months old. Even a fully-mature Devon may prove an excellent choice for some owners.

Kittens should not be obtained under 12 weeks old, though 14–16 weeks of age is better. No reputable breeder will sell them younger than this. Less caring breeders will let them go to new homes as young as eight weeks of age. Such juveniles will barely have been weaned. They will not have developed the needed resistance to major diseases. They are more likely to become stressed by the premature removal from their mother and siblings. Their vaccinations will not be fully effective. These factors will dramatically increase the risk of immediate problems.

SEX & COLOUR PATTERN

If it is to be purely a pet, the Devon's gender is unimportant. Both are delightful. Males are usually larger, bolder and more outgoing. Females tend to be more discerning about which humans

A kitten or adult Devon Rex can make a delightful pet for a cat lover. Regardless of the age of the cat, health and temperament are the main considerations when purchasing a Devon Rex.

they like. However, each Devon Rex is an individual. Its character and health, more than its sex, should be the basis of selection. Again, the sex is unimportant for the potential exhibitor. It is not even necessary for the cat to be sexually 'entire.' Classes for neuters are featured in shows.

Those with breeding aspirations are advised to obtain only females. All pet owners should regard neutering (males) and spaying (females) as obligatory. Today this can be effected at any age after eight weeks.

The colour is a matter of personal preference. It should never be placed ahead of health and character. Some colours and patterns will be available, and others will not. The more popular varieties may be less costly than the rarer ones. This would generally not apply to prospective breeding or exhibition individuals, where type quality will be more important than colour or pattern.

LOOK BEFORE YOU LEAP

It is important you meet as many Devon Rex breeders and kittens as you can. This gives you a good mental picture of what an healthy typical example should look like and cost for the quality and colour you want. Normally, you will get what you pay for. If you look for the cheapest kitten, there may be a sound reason

BONDING WITH THE DEVON REX

Lacking the full coat of typical cats, the Devon is quite happy to curl up on its owner's lap, or shoulder, to maintain warmth. Heavier-coated breeds, which means most in comparison to the Devon, will be less inclined to do this because they soon become too hot. The relative density of a cat's coat is thus another influence on the way it behaves.

If a cat spends much sleeping time with its owners, it will develop a stronger than normal bond with them. As a consequence, it will want to follow them around and get involved in all they do, irrespective of whether the owners actually want such assistance. Here we see the coat type as a motivator of behaviour.

Another factor that will promote close bonding with an owner is the unusual appearance of the Devon. It will tend to be owned by those who really do want to share their lives with their feline companion. Whenever this situation persists, the cat will quickly enough learn what little tricks gain lots of attention, such as paw waving. It will use these tricks often, as well as seeking others to add to its little repertoire. At the same time, the Devon owner will tend to notice all the little idiosyncrasies that might escape the attention of owners less bonded with their cats.

The colour pattern of your Devon Rex can range from solid black to pure white and a whole rainbow of colours in between. What colour is the most appealing to you?

AN HEALTHY KITTEN
Closely inspect any kitten before making a final decision. Keep in mind the following points:

Eyes and nose: Clean and clear with no signs of discharge.

Ears: Fresh-smelling and erect.

Coat: Healthy, not dull or dry.

Anal region: Clean with no staining of the fur.

Feet: Four toes on each foot, plus a dewclaw on the inside of each front leg.

Teeth: Correct bite.

There should be no signs of parasites or bald areas on the coat. A potbelly may indicate worms.

why it is the cheapest!

The best place to start your search is a cat show. At large cat shows, many colour varieties will be on display. Purchase the show catalogue. It lists all the exhibitors and their addresses. You can see if any live in your immediate locality. Whenever possible, it is best to purchase locally so you can visit the home of the breeder. Some will insist you do so in order to be satisfied that you will make a good owner.

Shows and breeders are advertised in the various cat magazines available from news agents. You can also contact a major cat registry, which will supply a list of national and regional clubs, which in turn are usually able to supply breeder lists. When visiting a breeder, always make an appointment. Try to visit no more than one cattery a day. This reduces the risk that you may transport pathogens (disease-causing organisms) from one establishment to the next. Selecting a good breeder is a case of noting the environment in which the cats are kept, the attitude of the owner to you and their cats, and how friendly and healthy the kittens look. It is vital that the chosen kitty has an outgoing personality. It must not appear timid or very shy. This indicates a lack of breeder sociali-sation or a genetic weakness in its temperament. Either way, it is not a kitten you should select.

CHOOSING A KITTEN
If you choose the breeder wisely, and especially if a friend recommends him, this will minimise problems related to your making a poor choice. However, a little knowledge on what to look for will not go amiss. Observe the

kittens from a distance to ensure none is unduly lethargic, which is never a good sign. If any kitten displays signs of illness, this should bring to an end any further thoughts of purchase from that source. A reputable breeder would not allow a sickly kitten to remain within its litter.

It is always advisable to select a kitten that shows particular interest in you. Devons are very discerning. If both of you are drawn to each other, this will greatly enhance the bonding essential for a strong relationship.

Once a particular kitten has been selected, it should be given a close physical inspection. The eyes and nose must show no signs of weeping or discharge. The ears will be erect and fresh smelling.

TAKING KITTY HOME

Arrange collection of the kitten as early in the day as possible. If a long journey is involved, be sure to take a few breaks so kitty does not suffer from travel sickness. Do not make stops to show the kitten to friends; this represents a health hazard. Once home, offer the kitten a drink, then allow it to sleep if it so requires. Children must be educated to handle a kitten gently, never to tease it and to respect its sleeping privacy. Until it is litter-trained, it should be restricted to the kitchen or another room with an easy-to-clean floor surface.

The coat should look healthy, never dry and dull. There must be no signs of parasites in the fur.

Most cats are comfortable with their litter boxes—though resting in them is not the best idea!

CAT LITTER

The litter that is used in cat boxes can be very variable, and in many cases cats reject the use of a cat box because of the litter. Certainly, if your cat rejects the use of the cat box, you should try different litters. You can start with the litters available at your local pet shop, then you can try sand, dirt, cedar shavings or whatever will appeal to your cat. Several cat owners grow clover in a tray and their cats seem to prefer that. However, the tray is kept outdoors and the cats may simply be marking the clover tray rather than using it for elimination purposes.

Your local pet shop will have scratching posts in various sizes and prices.

There will be no bald areas of fur, nor bodily swellings or abrasions. Lift the tail and inspect the anal region. This must be clean with no indication of congealed faecal matter. Any staining of the fur indicates current or recent diarrhoea.

The kitten must not display a potbelly. This may indicate worms or other internal disorders. Check the teeth to be sure of a correct bite. Bear in mind that the jawbones do not develop at the same rate. Minor imperfections may correct themselves (they may also get worse), but major faults will not. Inspect the feet to see there are four toes on each, plus a dewclaw on the inside of each front leg.

With respect to the colour, there is no link between this and health other than deafness in certain white varieties. Any faults in the colour or its placement will only be of importance in breeding or exhibition individuals. The potential breeder/exhibitor should obtain a copy of the official standard so they are *au fait* with all colour, pattern and bodily faults of the breed.

KITTY SHOPPING SPREE
Certain accessories should be regarded as obligatory and obtained before the kitten arrives at your home.

Your local pet shop should have an array of scratching posts that will delight your Devon Rex. Do not attempt to make a post yourself as many carpets are too weak to stand the tearing or may have been dyed with chemicals harmful to cats.

Your local pet shop should carry a full range of litter trays, litter boxes and tools with which you keep the box clean.

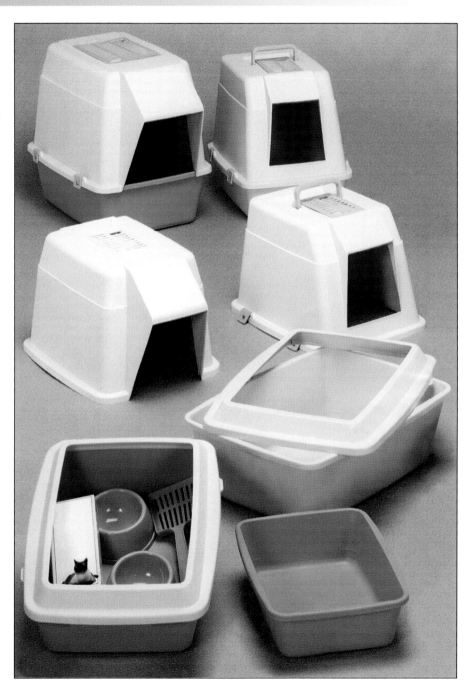

ADOPTING AN ADULT

Some owners, such as the elderly, may benefit by adopting an adult cat. They can avoid the demanding needs of a young kitten and enjoy the advantages of a well-trained adult. Breeders and exhibitors can also benefit from purchasing an older cat because it is easier to assess the quality. Sometimes, though, older cats can have bad habits that are hard to break. So if you are thinking about obtaining an older cat, it is important to thoroughly investigate possible behavioural and health problems.

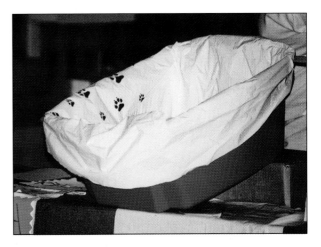

SCRATCHING POST

This will save the furniture from being abused! There are many models, some being simple posts, others are combined with play stations and sleeping quarters. These are the best.

LITTER BOX(ES)

Some are open trays; others are domed to provide extra privacy. Still others have special bases in which odour removers are fitted.

CAT LITTER

There are numerous types on the market, each offering advantages and presenting drawbacks. Avoid the low cost types that contain a lot of dangerous dust. Use those that are fully biodegradable.

FOOD/WATER DISHES

Polished metal has the longest wear life. Earthenware is less costly than metal and superior to the plastic types.

GROOMING TOOLS

These will comprise a good-quality bristle brush or grooming glove, a fine-toothed comb, nail trimmers and a soft chamois leather.

CAT COLLAR AND/OR HARNESS

Select elasticised collars. Be sure a name and address disc or barrel

Liners are available for most litter trays to assist in keeping them clean and more manageable.

Double-bowl feeders are very convenient for feeding your cat. Go to your pet shop to purchase top-quality feeders, which should come in a variety of colours, styles and sizes.

Cat toys are entertaining for cat and owner alike. Purchase toys that require interaction between you and your Devon Rex, thereby affording the cat exercise and companionship while playing.

Your local pet shop will have a variety of cat toys with which you can entertain your Devon Rex and yourself.

Cat carriers are a necessity of cat ownership, though no cat welcomes the opportunity of being carted about in a crate. Nonetheless, the carrier is the only safe option for transport to the veterinary surgeon.

is fitted to this. A harness must be a snug but comfortable fit if it is to be effective.

CARRYING BOX

This is essential for transporting the cat to the vet or other places, as well as for home restriction when needed. Be sure it is roomy enough to accommodate a fully-grown Devon Rex. The choice is between collapsible models, soft plastic types and, the best choice, those made of wood or fibreglass.

If you are considering walking your Devon Rex, you must have a lead that is suitable for a cat.

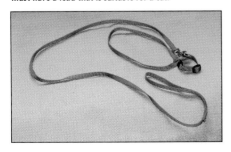

DEVON REX CAT

For a young Devon Rex, its human environment holds many dangers. Its owner must protect it from these until it becomes agile and wiser. The following dangers lurk in typical households. Check whether there are additional ones in your own home. The most important decision you need to make from the outset is whether or not the kitten is to be given outdoor liberty, which the author certainly does not recommend for the sparsely-coated Devon Rex.

HOW MUCH FREEDOM?

More than at any time in the past the question of how much freedom a cat should be given is the subject of heated debate. It is a very subjective matter. Here the more pertinent points are given so you can relate these to your home location. This, to a very large degree, should influence your decision.

Cats living in or close to an urban area are at the highest safety risk. The amount of traffic is such that death from road accidents is a major concern. In such environments there are high dog populations, some of which are dangerous to cats. Injury or death from dog attacks is therefore another major source of danger to a feline.

Urban cat populations are also extremely high. Far too many cats are living a virtually feral existence. These are tough, street-wise cats that often carry fleas and other parasites that are vectors of disease. Some will be carriers of, or infected with, feline leukaemia and other deadly diseases.

The typical feline family pet can be badly injured if it becomes engaged in fights with these roaming bullies. Furthermore, their very presence in and around a gentle cat's garden can cause the pet severe stress. This can make it fearful of stepping outside its home. In some instances, it may cause the pet to actually leave its home.

BE ONE JUMP AHEAD

Seemingly innocuous things, such as doors, can become life-threatening should they suddenly slam shut on a kitten due to a strong draught. When windows and external doors are open, be sure internal doors are secured with a doorstop. At all times be one jump ahead of a kitten in terms of identifying dangerous situations.

Sadly, if these risks are not enough, there is no shortage of people who will steal a pedigreed cat, the more so if it is friendly. Add to this the number of abusive people who do not like cats roaming into their gardens, and the scenario is not good. Finally, free-roaming cats also take a heavy toll on local bird and wildlife populations.

Taking these various facts into account, the urban cat is best kept indoors. It can enjoy the benefit of the outdoors if supplied with a roomy aviary-type exercise pen. Some cats can be trained to walk on a lead. This allows outdoor enjoyment, even if this is restricted to the garden. When walking your cat in public places, use only a harness. This is much safer than a collar.

In contrast to urban situations,

THE TRAVELLING CAT

Whenever your cat needs to be taken on a car journey, never let it travel loose in the vehicle, which is illegal. It must always be in its carrying box. If a cat were to go under the clutch or brake pedal when the car was moving, this would be dangerous to all occupants. A cat might also spring from one seat to another, which might distract the driver. This could have disastrous results.

Never leave a cat alone in a car on a hot day. The temperature can rise dramatically to the point that the cat is unable to breathe. It could die of heat stroke. Always leave a window partially open, but not so wide that the agile cat could escape.

THE GARAGE AND SHED

These two buildings are very dangerous to a kitten. Sharp and heavy tools, nails, glass jars, garden weed killers and open tins of paint are but a sampling of the items the average family uses or stores in these. A kitten may clamber into the engine compartment of a vehicle. This could be fatal if the owner happened to start the engine before the kitten had removed itself. Always know where the kitten is.

the cat living in a rural environment is far safer, the more so if there are no immediate neighbours or busy roads. Even so, it is wise to restrict the cat's outdoor freedom to daylight hours. During the night it is more likely to get run over or to threaten local wildlife.

Those living between the extremes of isolated areas and

DANGEROUS DISINFECTANTS

Although owners should disinfect the litter box regularly to prevent disease and illness, some household disinfectants can be harmful to cats. Pine-oil-based cleaners are toxic to cats. DO NOT use them. Products containing Phenol should also be avoided. Bleach is a good disinfectant to use; however, be sure to rinse the litter box thoroughly and air it out to get rid of any fumes.

busy urban environments should consider the local risk factor. Generally it is best to keep the cat indoors but to provide an outdoor exercise pen.

HOUSEHOLD DANGERS

Within its home, a kitten is best viewed as an accident waiting to happen! The most dangerous room is the kitchen. Hot electric hobs, naked flames from gas rings, boiling pans of food or water, and sinks full of water are obvious hazards. An iron left on its board with cable trailing to the floor is an invitation to a kitten to jump up—with potentially fatal consequences. Washing machines or spin dryers with warm clothes in them and their doors open are inviting places to nap. Always check the kitty isn't inside if the door has been left open.

Cupboards containing poisonous or other dangerous substances should always be kept securely closed.

In the living room, the normal dangers are aquariums without hoods, unguarded fires, electric bar heaters, poisonous indoor plants, trailing electrical wires, and ornaments that may be knocked over by a mischievous kitty. Toilets can be fatal to an over-curious kitten. The same is true of a bath containing water. Balconies should be safeguarded to remove the potential for the kitten to slip and fall.

OTHER DANGERS

Other potential dangers are when electric tools are left lying about

BOARDING YOUR CAT

Cats do not like to travel and the best alternative is to have a trusted friend, relative or pet-sitter watch your cat in your home. If this is impossible, then you may have to board your cat. You can get recommendations from friends or your veterinary surgeon as to which catteries are reputable. When choosing a boarding house, you should visit the facility beforehand to make certain that it is clean and quiet, and that the personnel are caring and attentive to boarders. You should also enquire about their policies concerning health, vaccinations and neutering.

and connected to power outlets—even worse if they are left on, as with bench saws. If the kitten is given freedom to exercise in a garden containing a pond, the kitten must be under constant supervision. Cherished ornaments should be placed out of reach of the kitten, as much for their safety as to any danger they may present to the kitty. It's not always the direct danger of something that can be the problem. If an ornament or similar item crashes to the floor, this can startle the kitten into a panicked departure! The kitten could then fall from a shelf in its hasty retreat.

Whether indoors or out, you must keep a close eye on your Devon Rex kitten, whose curiosity and energy could get it into trouble.

Feeding Your
DEVON REX CAT

Today the feeding of cats has been reduced to its most simple level with the availability of many scientifically prepared commercial diets. However, this fact can result in owners' becoming casual in their approach to the subject. While the main object of a given diet is to provide the ingredients that promote healthy growth and maximum immunity to disease, it also fulfils an important secondary role.

A proper diet must maintain in the cat a psychological feeling of well-being that avoids

nutritionally related stress problems or syndromes. By ensuring the diet is balanced, of good variety and never monotonous, these dual roles will be achieved. This approach will also avoid the situation of the cat's becoming a finicky eater.

BALANCE AND VARIETY
A balanced diet means one that contains all of the major ingredients—protein, fats, carbohydrates, vitamins and minerals—in the ratios needed to ensure maximum

growth and health. Variety means supplying foods in a range of forms that will maintain and stimulate the cat's interest in its meals. Commercially formulated foods come in three levels of moisture: low (dried), semi-moist and moist (tinned).

Generally, the dried and tinned forms are the most popular. Dried cat foods have the advantage that they can be left in the cat dish for longer periods of time than can tinned foods. They are ideal for supplying on a free-choice basis. Like the tinned varieties, they come in a wide range of popular flavours.

In order to meet the specific needs of a kitten, there are specially formulated foods available. These contain higher protein levels needed by a growing kitten. As it grows, the kitten can be slowly weaned onto the adult types. There are also special brands available from vets for any kitten or cat that may have a dietary problem as well as special diets for the older cat. These may need lower ratios of certain ingredients, such as proteins and sodium, so as to reduce the workload of the liver.

Flavours should be rotated so interest in meals is maintained. This also encourages familiarity with different tastes. Naturally, a Devon Rex will display a greater liking for certain flavours and brands than for others.

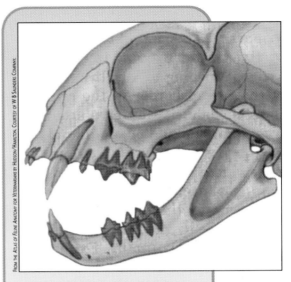

FROM THE ATLAS OF FELINE ANATOMY FOR VETERINARIANS BY HUDSON/HAMILTON, COURTESY OF W B SAUNDERS COMPANY.

MEET THE MEAT-EATERS

Since cats are carnivorous, their teeth are designed to bite and cut. Except for crunching dried foods, cats do very little chewing. They have the fewest teeth of any common domestic mammal—typically 30 (although there are some variations). The canines usually are more developed than the incisors.

FRESH FOODS

To add greater variety and interest, there are many fresh foods that a Devon Rex will enjoy. Some will be very helpful in cleaning the teeth and exercising the jaw muscles. All have the benefit of providing different textures and smells that help stimulate the palate. Feed these foods two or three times a week as

IMPORTANT DON'TS

- Do not let your cat become a fussy eater. Cats are not born fussy, but are made that way by their owners. Your cat will not starve if given the correct food, but it may try to convince you otherwise. However, a cat that refuses all foods offered may be ill. Contact your vet.
- Do not give a cat sweet and sticky foods. These provide no benefit and, if eaten, will negatively affect normal appetite for wholesome foods.
- Do not feed vitamin and mineral supplements to either kittens or adults unless under advice from a veterinary surgeon. Excess vitamins and minerals can be as bad for your cat's health as a lack of them. They will create potentially dangerous cellular metabolic imbalances.
- Do not give any questionable foods, such as those that smell or look 'off.' If in doubt, discard them. Always store foods in cool, darkened cupboards. Be sure all foods from the freezer and refrigerator are fully thawed.

treats or occasionally as complete meals.

Cooked poultry, including the skin, but minus the bones, is usually a favourite, as is quality raw or cooked mincemeat. Cooked beef on the bone gives the cat something to enjoy. Cooked white fish, as well as tinned tuna or sardines, is an example of an ocean delight. Never feed raw fish; this can prove dangerous, even fatal. Although cats rarely enjoy items such as rice, pasta or cooked vegetables, these can nonetheless be finely chopped and mixed with meats or fish. Some Devons may develop a taste for them. Various cheeses and scrambled or boiled eggs will often be appreciated—but never give raw eggs.

If the diet is balanced and varied, the addition of vitamin and mineral supplements is unnecessary and can actually prove dangerous. While certain of these compounds are released from the body if in excess, others are not. They are stored and can adversely affect efficient metabolism. If a cat shows loss of condition and disinterest in its food, discuss its diet with your vet.

HOW MUCH TO FEED

Food intake is influenced by many factors. These are the cat's age, activity level, the ambient temperature (more is eaten in the colder months), the cat's

Offer your Devon Rex a top-quality cat food, available from your pet shop. Cats usually do not overeat, so you do not have to worry too much about offering too much.

> ### DRIED FOOD— MORE WATER
> If the cat is only given dried foods, it is essential that its water bowl is always full; it will need to drink more. But it is best to give both dried and moist food types. This minimises the risk of urological problems created by pH alkalinity associated with dried diets.

four meals a day. When the kitten is six months old, one meal can be dropped. By twelve months of age, only two meals will be required, possibly only one if dried foods are also available on a free-choice basis. As the number of meals is decreased, the quantity must be increased at the meals offered.

FOOD AND WATER CONTAINERS

Devons are not too fussy over what vessels are used for supplying their food and water, but a few tips are useful. Devons do not like to eat from dirty dishes anymore than you would. Their food bowls should be

Feed your Devon Rex in a quiet area free of walking traffic, a place where the cat feels comfortable and safe.

breeding state (rearing kittens) and the quality of the food. Always follow the breeder's recommendations on diet until your kitten has settled into your home. Thereafter the needed quantity will increase as the kitten gets older, until full maturity at about two to three years of age.

As a basic guide, a four-month-old kitten will require

> ### HIGH-QUALITY FOOD
> The value of a cat food is determined by its protein/carbohydrate compositions. High-quality foods will contain more protein. The cat is a prime predator and needs a high proportion of protein in its diet.

washed after each meal. Water containers should be washed and replenished every day. Saucers make ideal food plates. Wide feeders from your pet shop are excellent for dried biscuits. Pottery or polished metal containers are better investments than plastic. They last longer and are easier to keep clean.

Having a short muzzle, the Devon Rex does not like to place its head into deep food dishes nor do they like their whiskers to touch the inner walls. Ensure dishes are wide and shallow.

WHERE AND WHEN TO FEED

Usually, the best place to feed a cat is in the kitchen or a low-

ESTABLISHING DAILY INTAKE

Quoting amounts needed is impossible because of the varying factors mentioned. The best way to establish requirements is on an actual consumption basis. Place a small amount of food on the dish and see how quickly this is eaten. If all is devoured within a few minutes, add a little more. Repeat this until the kitten/cat is satiated and walks away from its dish. Do likewise at the other meals and you will quickly establish daily intake.

traffic utility area. It is important to place food and water dishes as far away from the litter tray as possible. This could otherwise deter the cat from eating. Cats also like to eat in quiet comfort. Meals should be spread across the entire day. When the number is reduced to two, these should be given in the morning and evening at convenient times. For the Devon Rex given outdoor freedom, it is best to feed the main meal in the evening. This encourages it to come home at this time. It can then be kept indoors overnight.

DEVON REX CAT

Over-zealous grooming of the Devon Rex can be detrimental. The loosely rooted guard hairs of the breed's unique coat might be damaged unless the brush is judiciously applied. The following information is provided as a general guide but should be used sparingly in the instances of brushing and bathing.

BRUSHING

Place the cat on a table of a height enabling you to comfortably control and groom the kitty. It can be useful to place white paper on the table. If any fleas are present, you will more easily notice them if they are groomed out of the fur. If the grooming is carried out gently, cats enjoy the experience. You should start when your Devon Rex is still a kitten. Commence by brushing the fur on the back of the neck. Work along the back and down the sides, then down the legs and finally the tail. The abdominal area must be brushed more gently as it is very sensitive.

Next, repeat the process using the fine-toothed comb. Then comb against the lie of the hair. This will enable you to see if there are any parasites present. These often favour the tail base or the neck behind the ears. Next, comb with the lie of the fur. Add a final lustre by brushing with the chamois.

BATHING

Occasionally, even Devon Rex Cats may need bathing. This may be of the wet or dry type. For wet baths, using the kitchen sink is preferable to a bath. This saves bending and allows for better control of the cat. To prevent the cat from sliding, use a rubber mat. A spray attachment is more efficient than a jug to wet and rinse the coat. The cat should have its own towels.

The choice of shampoo is important. It should ideally be formulated for cats—do not use one for dogs, which could cause problems on a cat's coat. Baby shampoos are the best alternative. Dry shampoos in powder form are available from pet shops. Alternatives would be talcum powder, powdered chalk or heated bran flakes.

The kitten should be bathed

Some Devon Rex owners prefer to use a grooming glove on the cat's coat instead of a traditional brush. The cat's coat is very sensitive and too much brushing can cause the cat harm.

HAIRBALLS (Trichobezoar)

When cats self-groom, they invariably swallow some of their hairs. Normally these do not create a problem. However, if many dead hairs are in the coat, these may be licked and swallowed to accumulate in the stomach as hairballs. These are more common in longhaired breeds than in those with short hair. Hairballs may create intestinal blockages that may so irritate the cat's intestinal tract that it vomits the hairball or voids it via its faecal matter.

If the hairball is not removed, and the cat displays reduced appetite, veterinary assistance is needed. Regular grooming greatly reduces the risk of this condition. Additionally, a teaspoon of liquid paraffin or other laxative once a week may be helpful in cats prone to this problem. A laxative, however, is unlikely to remove an existing hairball. Pineapple juice containing the enzyme bromelain may break down small furballs. One teaspoonful a day for three days is the recommended dosage.

by the time it is six months of age. This will familiarise it with the process before it matures and the process degenerates into a pitched battle. Cats have no love of bathing but can come to accept it if it does not become an unpleasant ordeal.

Grooming should always precede bathing, as this will remove any dead hairs. The key to success lies in ensuring that no water or shampoo is allowed to enter and irritate the eyes or ears. You should be able to cope single-handedly with a kitten. However, it may be prudent to have someone else present just in case the adult proves more of a super cat than a kitten!

The water temperature should be warm, never cold or too hot. Prepare a shampoo and water solution before commencing. Have a large towel at hand. Commence by soaking the fur of the neck, then work along the back, sides, legs and tail. Pour shampoo onto the back and work this in all directions until the cat has been fully shampooed. Next, thoroughly rinse all the shampoo away. It is essential that none be left, otherwise it may cause later irritation. Gently but firmly squeeze all water from the coat. The face can be cleaned using a dampened flannel.

Wrap the kitten in the towel and give it a brisk rubbing until it is as dry as possible. It can then be allowed to dry naturally, after which it can be given a final brush and polish. If the cat is normally allowed outdoors, do not allow this for some hours until you are sure the coat is dry. In the colder months it is best to attend to bathing in the early evening and keep the cat indoors overnight. The use of a hand dryer is not essential on a short-coated breed, but does shorten the drying time.

EARS, EYES AND NAILS

When inspecting the ears, look for any signs of dirt. This can be gently wiped away using a dampened cotton bud or one with just a little baby or vegetable oil on it. Never attempt to probe into the ear. If the ear is very waxed, this may indicate any of various health problems. A visit to the vet is recommended. The corner of the eyes can be gently wiped with damp cotton wool to remove any dust that occasionally accumulates.

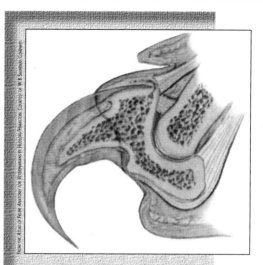

FROM THE ATLAS OF FELINE ANATOMY FOR VETERINARIANS BY HUDSON/HAMILTON, COURTESY OF W B SAUNDERS COMPANY.

PRESS-ON NAILS!

A stylish and fairly successful inhibitor of scratching is a plastic covering on the nails. A plastic sheath is placed over each nail and glued on with a strong, permanent adhesive. Depending upon the cat's activity, these sheaths last from one to three months.

DECLAWING

Declawing is the surgical removal of all of the claw (or nail) and the first toe joint. This practice is heavily frowned upon and even illegal in some countries, such as the United Kingdom. Unfortunately, in some areas of the world this procedure is still performed. Some owners only have the claws from the front feet removed; others do all four feet. An alternative surgical procedure is removing the tendon that allows the cat to protract its claws. This procedure, referred to as a tendonectomy, as compared to an onychectomy (removal of the claws), is less traumatic for the cat. Claws still must be filed and trimmed after a tendonectomy.

Declawing is not always 100% successful. In two-thirds of the cases, the cats recovered in 72 hours. Only 4–5% of the cats hadn't recovered within a fortnight. About 3% of the cats had their claws grow back!

GINGIVITIS (Plasmocytic-Lymphocytic Stomatitis)

There are many causes of this condition. But the end result is the same—bad breath, excessive plaque, tooth loss and, almost certainly, pain. The cat salivates excessively, starts to eat less and consequently loses weight. On inspection, the gums are swollen, especially in the area of the premolar and molar teeth. They bleed easily. There are various treatments, such as antibiotics, immunostimulants and disinfectant mouth gels. However, these invariably prove short-term and merely delay the inevitable treatment of extraction.

Prevention avoids this painful condition. Regular tooth inspection and cleaning, plus provision of hard-food items, such as cat biscuits, achieve this to a large extent. There are also special cat chews made of dried fish that help clean the teeth. They also contain antibacterial enzymes that minimise or prevent secondary bacteria from accumulating. Ask for these at your pet shop or vet's surgery. Gingivitis may commence in kittens, so do not think it is something that only occurs in older cats.

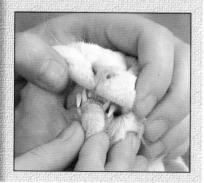

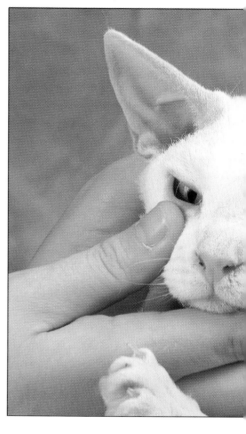

Inspection of a cat's claws is achieved by firstly restraining the cat while on its back on your lap or held against your chest. Hold the paw and apply pressure to the top of this with your thumb. The nail will appear from its sheath. If the nail needs trimming, use the appropriate trimmers.

It is vital that you do not cut into, or even too close to, the quick, which is a blood vessel. This can be seen as a darker area of the nail in pink-clawed cats. It

is more difficult, or not possible, to see the quick in dark-coloured nails. In such instances, trim less. You may need a helper to do the trimming or the holding. If in doubt, let your vet do this for you. If cats have ample access to scratching posts, they will only infrequently, if ever, require their nails to be trimmed.

Pay particular attention to your Devon's eyes. Wipe any accumulated dust from the cat's eye area.

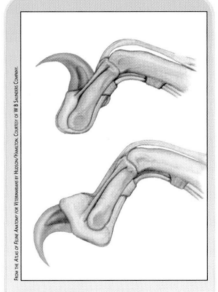

FROM THE *ATLAS OF FELINE ANATOMY FOR VETERINARIANS* BY HUDSON/HAMILTON. COURTESY OF W B SAUNDERS COMPANY.

Never probe into the cat's ear. Use a dampened cotton bud to remove visible debris.

RETRACTABLE CLAWS

When at rest, a cat's claws are retracted. The muscles hold the claws in their sheaths. The claw is then extended if the cat wishes to attack prey, defend itself, grab an object or climb. That is why your cat's claws are not always visible. This is true for all species of felines except the cheetah, which is unable to retract its claws, except when it is very young.

TEETH

From its youngest days, your kitten should become familiar with having its teeth cleaned. Many owners do not give these the attention they should. This has become progressively more important due to the soft diet regimens of modern cats. Initially, gently rub the kitten's teeth using a soft cloth on which cat toothpaste has been placed. This will accustom the kitten to having its teeth touched as well as to the taste of the tooth cleaner. When this is no problem for the kitten, you can progress to a soft toothbrush and ultimately one of medium hardness. Periodically let your vet check the cat's mouth.

CLEAN CATS

Cats are self-groomers. They use their barbed tongues and front paws for grooming. Some cats never groom themselves, while others spend up to a third of their waking hours grooming themselves. Licking stimulates certain skin glands that make the coat waterproof.

If gently applied, a grooming glove can be used to remove debris from the Devon's coat.

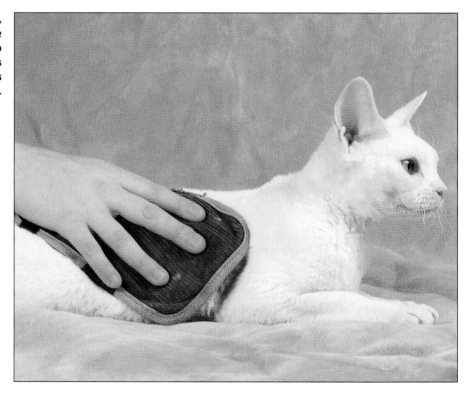

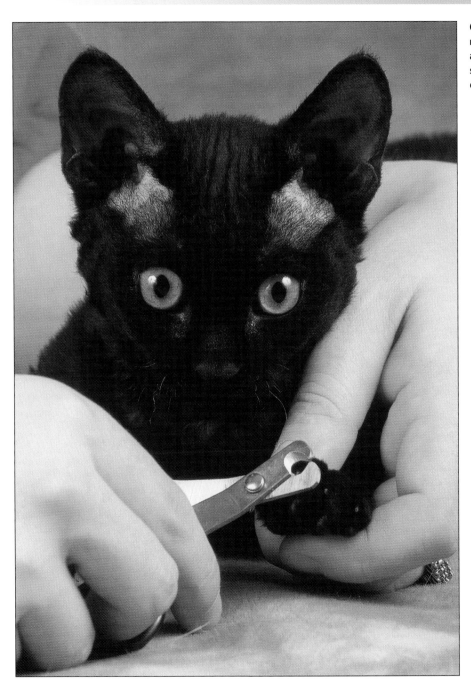

Clipping a Devon's nails will limit the amount of scratching the cat does indoors.

One of the outstanding virtues of cats is that they are easy to live with. They are fastidious in their personal habits related to grooming and toilet routines and basically require very little of their owners. Nonetheless, behavioural problems in cats can occur, and an owner needs to understand all the possible causes and solutions. You may never encounter a single problem with your Devon Rex, but it pays to be prepared should your feline charge disrupt your domestic bliss.

THE BASIS OF TRAINING
The most effective means of training a cat is via reinforcement of success. A cat learning from lavish praise of doing what is required will want to repeat the action to gain more affection. There are no potential negative side effects. Conversely, when scolding or another method of discipline is used, there is always the possibility that the cat will not relate the punishment to what the owner had intended.

For example, you cannot discipline for something done in the past. The past is anything much longer than a few minutes

SETTING THE GROUND RULES
From the outset you must determine the ground rules and stick to them. Always remember that your companion's patterns of behaviour begin to form from the moment it first arrives at your home. If the future adult is not to be given outdoor freedom, then do not let it outdoors as a kitten. If any rooms are to be out of bounds to the adult, then do not let the kitten into them. Stability is vital in a cat's life; without it, the result will be stress and its related behavioural changes.

Ground rules of how to handle the kitten and to respect its privacy when sleeping should be instilled into all children. The cat's meals should be given at about the same time each day. This will have the secondary advantage that the pet's toilet habits will be more predictable.

The Devon Rex is a most alert and attentive cat, which may be more responsive to training than many other cat breeds.

ago. If you call the cat to you and punish it for something done hours earlier, it cannot relate to

CATS AND OTHER PETS

If you already have a pet cat or cats, or dogs, or almost any other animal that isn't small, creeping or crawling, your cat can usually be socialised so the other pet and the cat will tolerate each other. In many cases, cats and dogs become quite friendly and attached to each other, often making frequent physical contacts, sleeping together or even sharing each other's food.

that action. It will relate the discipline to the act of going to you when called! This will create insecurity in the pet, increasing the risk that more problems will develop.

REMEDIAL METHODS

When faced with a problem, firstly try to pinpoint the likely cause(s). Next, consider the remedial options. Be sure these will not result in negative side effects linked to you. Always be the paragon of patience. Some problems may be extremely complex and deeply rooted within the cat's behaviour patterns. As such, they are habits not easily changed, and often difficult to analyse. In discussing the following problems, it is hoped that you will understand the basic ways to correct other unwanted patterns of behaviour that might occur. But always remember that it is far better to avoid a problem than correct it.

THE LITTER TRAY
A very common problem for some owners is that their cat starts to attend to its toiletry needs anywhere other than in its litter tray. The problem may become apparent from the time the kitten gets to its new home, or it may develop at any time during its life. So, let us start from the beginning and try to avoid the situation.

Until you are satisfied that the kitten is using its litter tray, do not give it access to carpeted rooms. The youngster should already have been litter trained well before you obtained it. You should buy a litter tray similar to the one it is already familiar with. It is also important that the same brand of litter is used, at least initially. Place the tray in a quiet spot so the kitten has privacy when attending to its needs.

A kitten will need to relieve itself shortly after it has eaten, exercised, or been sleeping. Watch it carefully at these times. If it stoops to attend to its needs other than in the litter tray, calmly lift it

CAUSES OF LITTER-BOX PROBLEMS
1. The litter tray is dirty. Cats never like to use a previously fouled tray.
2. The litter has been changed to one of a different texture that the cat does not like. Generally the finer-grained litters are the most favoured.
3. A scented litter is being used to mask odours. The cat may not like the scent. Such litters should not be necessary if the tray is regularly cleaned.
4. The tray is regularly cleaned, but an ammonium or pine-based disinfectant is being used. This may aggravate the cat's sensitive nasal mucous membranes. Additionally, the phenols in pine are dangerous to cats.
5. The litter tray is located too close to the cat's food and water bowls. Cats do not like to eat near litter trays or to defecate/urinate close to their feeding areas.
6. Another cat or free-roaming pet has been added to the household and is causing the cat stress. In multi-cat households, two or more trays may be needed.
7. There is insufficient litter in the tray. There should be about 2 inches of litter depth.
8. The cat has developed a fear of using the tray due to an upsetting experience. For instance, the owner may have caught the cat as it finished using the tray in order that it could be given a medicine. Children may be disturbing it while it is relieving itself.
9. The cat is ill (or elderly) and is unable to control its bowel movements. Veterinary attention is required.
10. The cat, because of one or more of the previous problems, has established other more favourable areas.

into its tray and scratch at the litter. Never shout or panic the kitty by making a sudden rush for it. If it does what is hoped, give it lots of praise. If it steps out of the tray without relieving itself, gently place it back in for a few seconds.

If nothing happens, be patient and wait, then repeat the process. If it fouls the kitchen floor when you are not watching, simply clean this up and wait for the next opportunity to transport the kitten to its tray. It rarely takes long for a kitten to consistently use this. Be very sure the tray is kept spotless. Cats have no desire to use a fouled toilet. Every few days, give the cat tray a good wash using soapy water and always rinse it thoroughly. Allow it to dry, then fill the tray with litter to depth of about 4–5 cms (1.5–2 inches).

By identifying the cause(s) of litter-box problems, the correction is often self-evident. However, correcting the cause is only part of the solution. Next, the habit of fouling other places must be overcome. Where possible, do not let the cat enter rooms it has started to foul until the odour has had time to fully disperse. Wash the area of the accident, then treat carpets and soft furnishings with an odour neutraliser (not an air freshener) from your pet shop or vet.

If the cat cannot be prevented from entering certain rooms, then cover previously fouled areas with plastic sheeting or tinfoil, or rinse the fouled area with white vinegar (which cats hate!). Also, place a litter tray in the fouled room while the retraining is underway. It may, help if a different size, type, or colour of tray is used.

SCENT MARKING

Both sexes scent mark, though males are more prolific. It is a means of advertising their presence in a territory, thus an integral part of their natural

TIDY TOILETING

During the kitten's stay in the nest box, the mother will assist or even stimulate bowel and urine elimination, at least for the first month of the kitten's life. The mother also does the clean-up work in the nest box. But once the kitten is older, it becomes capable of relieving itself out of the nest box. Usually the kitten likes sand, soft earth or something that seems absorbent and is easily moved with its paws. By the time the kitten is two months old, it should develop the discipline of covering its elimination. Not all kittens develop this discipline, though the use of an absorbent clay litter seems to be helpful in developing this discipline in young cats. Your local pet shop will have various cat litters to offer you..

FERAL CATS

Feral cats are, as a general rule, undernourished. They spend most of their time searching for food. Consequently, those feral cats that have kittens spend less time with their kittens than do well-nourished cats. It has been shown that kittens born to feral mothers are usually unsocial and show little affection for their mothers. Obviously, they would show a similar lack of affection for a human. That's one of the reasons that feral kittens make poor pets and should neither be adopted nor brought into your home. Kittens, which for any reason are separated from their mothers at the age of two weeks, develop an attitude of fear and wariness. They escape from contact with other cats or humans and can even be dangerous if they feel trapped.

behaviour. Spraying is usually done against a vertical surface. It tells other males that the individual is residing in that territory. Alternatively, it will tell a female that a male lives close by—or, with a female, it will tell the male that a female is in the area. It is thus a very important part of a cat's social language.

Neutered cats have little need to mark their territory or leave their 'calling card' to attract mates. They are far less likely to spray than those not altered.

However, scent marking may commence when the cat is attempting to assert its position in the household.

To overcome the problem of scent marking, you first try and identify if there is an obvious specific cause. In multi-cat households, it also requires positive identification of the sprayer(s) and the favoured spraying surface. Giving the cat more freedom may help, and its own sleeping place if it does not have one. Covering the sprayed surface with plastic sheeting, or a cloth impregnated with a scent the cat does not like (such as lemon, pepper or bleach), may be successful. Spraying the cat with a water pistol when catching it in the action is a common ploy. Veterinary treatment with the hormone progesterone may prove effective—discuss this with your vet.

SCRATCHING
Scratching is a normal feline characteristic. Unfortunately, house cats tend to destroy the furniture to satisfy their need to scratch. Feral or outdoor cats usually attack a tree because trees are readily accessible and the bark of the tree suits their needs perfectly. If the outdoor cat lives in a pride, it will scratch more than a solitary feral cat. The reasons for this are known. When cats scratch, they leave telltale

marks. Parts of the nail's sheath exudate from glands located between their claws, and the visual aspects are the marks that cats leave to impress or advertise their presence.

Cat owners should not consider their cats' scratching as an aggressive behavioural disorder. It is normal for cats to scratch. Keeping your cat's claws clipped or filed so they are as short as possible without causing bleeding may inhibit scratching. Your vet can teach you how to do this. Clipping and filing should be started when the kitten is very young. Starting this when the cat has matured is much more difficult and may even be dangerous.

There are ways to control annoying cat scratching. Certainly, the easiest way is to present your cat with an acceptable cat scratching post. These are usually available at most local pet shops. The post should be covered with a material that is to your cat's liking. If your cat has already indicated what it likes to scratch, it usually is a good idea to acquire a post covered with this same material. Veterinary surgeons often suggest sandpaper, as this will reduce the cat's nails quickly and the cat will not have the urge to scratch. Certainly using hemp, carpeting, cotton towelling or bark is worth a try. Once the cat uses the post, it usually will have

MAN MEETS CAT

Early man, perhaps 8000 years ago, started his symbiotic relationship with domestic cats, *Felis catus* or *Felis domesticus*. The cats killed and ate the rats and mice and probably anything else which crawled and was small, which early man attracted and considered as pests. Early man reciprocated by allowing the cat to sleep in his cave, hut or tent. Cats, being essentially nocturnal, kept the small mammals (rats, mice, etc.) from disturbing the sleep of early man.

As early man evolved to modern man, the domestic cat came along as an aid to pest control. This was especially true of peoples who farmed, as farmers were plagued with rodents. Though most cats were not selectively bred for their predatory skills, it was obvious that those cats that were the best hunters were more successful in evolutionary terms than the cats that were more meek. Modern cats have changed very little from the cats from which they descended. There are still, today, cats that are very predatory, attacking small mammals and birds; there are also meek cats which, unless fed by their owners, would perish in a competitive cat society.

It has been shown repeatedly that if kittens are socialised in a proper manner, they will become peaceful pets. This includes lions and tigers. If the kittens are not socialised properly, they revert immediately to their aggressive, predatory behaviours.

CAUSES OF SCENT MARKING

1. Another cat, or pet, has been introduced to the household. It may be bullying the resident cat. This problem may resolve itself when the two get to know each other. The more cats there are, the longer it may take for the situation to be resolved. Much will depend on the space within which the cats may roam and whether they are able to avoid those they dislike.
2. The birth of a new family member may annoy the cat for a while, especially if its owner suddenly gives it less attention.
3. A friend staying in the home for a few days may not like cats. If 'shooed' away a number of times, the cat may feel it should assert its position and mark it.
4. If the cat is given outdoor freedom, a bully may have moved into the territory. Having lost control of its own garden, the pet may assert its territorial boundaries within its home. If a cat flap is used, another cat may be entering the home and this will trigger the resident to scent mark.

cats prefer semi-darkness. Some prefer flat surfaces and not vertical surfaces. Some prefer public areas in which their human friends are present instead of secluded areas. It may be stress-related, as with scent marking, because scratching is another territorial marking behaviour. In any case, the idea is to get your cat to scratch the post and not the carpets, furniture, drapes or duvet on your bed.

CAT SCRATCH DISEASE

An objectionable habit of many poorly raised kittens is their exuberant jumping to greet you. This flying jump may result in the kitten's being attached to your body; otherwise it will fall to the floor and may injure itself. In the attachment process, your skin will usually be pierced, and this is a health concern. All cat scratches and bites should be thoroughly cleaned with an antiseptic soap. If a sore appears at the site of the wound, you should visit your family doctor immediately.

Cat scratch disease is a well-known problem. It is caused by a bacterium *(Rochalimaea henselae)* that is usually easily treated with antibiotics. However, more and more cases show resistance to the usual antibiotics.

Untreated cat scratch fever may result in an enlargement of the lymph nodes, imitating a cancerous condition known as lymphoma. The bottom line is that cat scratches should be taken seriously.

neither a desire nor a need to scratch any place else.

Besides the physical need to scratch, many cats have a psychological need to scratch. This is evidenced by where they scratch versus what they scratch. Often

Introduce your cat to the post by rubbing its paws on the post, hoping it will take the hint. Oftentimes the cat voluntarily attacks the post. Unfortunately, sometimes it doesn't. If you catch your cat scratching in a forbidden area, startle it with a loud shout, banging a folded newspaper against your hand, or something else which will take its attention away from scratching. Never hit the cat. This will only get a defensive reaction that might be counter-productive.

RUBBISH RUMMAGING

Cats are inquisitive and may decide to have a good look through any interesting rubbish bins that are exuding an enticing odour. Normally, the answer is to remove the bin. However, if the attraction always seems to be kitchen rubbish, there may be a nutritional problem. It may be searching for food because it is being underfed! It may alterna-tively be receiving an unbalanced diet and is trying to satisfy its inner need for a given missing ingredient.

Another possibility, and one that may be more appropriate to the indoors-only cat, is boredom or loneliness. These conditions can only be remedied by greater interaction between owner and cat and/or obtaining a companion feline.

Clearly the cause should be identified. The immediate solution is to place the rubbish in a cupboard or similar place that is out of the cat's reach. This type of solution is called removal of the re-enforcer. It is a common method of overcoming problems across a number of unwanted behaviours. However, it does not correct the underlying problem that must still be addressed.

The first-time cat owner should not think that the problems discussed will likely be encountered. They are only met when the cat's environment is lacking in some way. Always remember that the older cat may have problems with bowel control. An extra litter tray at another location in the home will usually remedy this situation. Finally, if a problem is found and you are not able to remedy it, do seek the advice of your vet or breeder.

Training your Devon to use a litter box doesn't usually require more than a proper introduction and correct placement of the box.

Breeding the Devon Rex is not within the capabilities and budgets of most pet owners. The following information is offered on the basis of general knowledge.

While the idea of becoming a breeder may appeal to many owners, the reality is more difficult than is often appreciated. It requires dedication, considerable investment of time and money, and the ability to cope with many heart-wrenching decisions and failures.

It would be quite impossible to discuss the complexities of practical breeding in only one chapter, so we will consider the important requirements of being a breeder plus some basic feline reproductive information. This will enable you to better determine if, indeed, this aspect of the hobby is for you.

BEING A BREEDER
Apart from great affection for the breed, a successful breeding programme requires quantifiable objectives. Foremost among these is the rearing of healthy kittens free from known diseases. Next is the desire to produce offspring that are as good as, indeed better than, their parents.

Such objectives ensure that a breeder will endeavour to maintain standards and reduce or remove from the breed population any instances of dangerous diseases and conditions. Only stock registered and tested free of major diseases should ever be used. Adopting such a policy helps to counteract those who breed from inferior and often unhealthy cats.

To be a successful breeder, you will need to become involved in the exhibition side of the hobby. Only via this route will you be able to determine if your programme is successful or not. Always remember that even the top-winning breeders still produce quite a high percentage of kittens that will only be of pet quality. There will be many

ROAMING ROMEOS
Males cats, toms, have extended testicles very early in life. By about nine months of age, the tom is capable of mating with a queen. Both queens and toms are polygamous and it is not uncommon for a queen to have a litter containing kittens fathered by different toms.

disappointments along the road to even modest success.

THE DISADVANTAGES OF BREEDING

There are many rewards to be gained from breeding but the disadvantages should also be carefully considered. Kittens are demanding, especially once they are over three weeks of age. Rearing, vaccination, registration and veterinary bills will be costly. Any thoughts of profit should be dispelled. Homes must be found for the kittens, which will entail receiving many telephone calls—some at very inconvenient hours.

Many potential buyers will prove to be either unsuitable or 'time wasters' looking for the cheapest pedigreed cat obtainable. Kittens may die, while cats of any age could test positive for a major disease. They may have to be put to sleep or given to a caring person who understands the particular problem.

Owning a number of cats will mean investing in cat pens. When females come into heat, they will try to escape and mate with any local tom with a twinkle in his eye! Their scent and calls will attract roving Romeos who will gather near your home and involve themselves in a series of raucous battles. Holidays and matings will need to be planned around hoped-for litter dates. All in all, owning even one or two

TOO MANY CATS

There are already too many cats in the world. In many countries, thousands of pathetic-looking felines can be seen wandering the streets in a badly emaciated state. They live tormented lives and have become a major social problem in many areas. There can be no excuse for these feral populations in developed Western nations. Quite frankly, some people who own cats, including some pedigreed owners, lack a sense of responsibility.

Cats allowed to roam in a non-neutered state are by far the main reason for the overpopulation problem. Unless a cat is of show or breeding quality, there is not a single justification for it to be bred or to remain in a non-neutered state. If your cat was purchased as a pet, you should help to resolve this global problem by having it neutered at the earliest possible date. This will make it a far healthier, happier and less problematic pet.

Rearing a litter of kittens is but one of a breeder's concerns. Many important decisions are made before the mating even takes place.

TOM FOOLERY

A non-neutered male cat kept as a single pet has little or no value for breeding purposes. It must be exhibited so it can gain some fame. The owner must have modern facilities to house both males and females. Females are always serviced at the home of the stud owner. This is extra responsibility and cost.

Such a male cannot be given any freedom to roam. If the tom is kept indoors, its scent-marking odours will often become intolerable. Even kept outdoors in a suitable cat pen, it will spray regularly to attract the attention of any females in the area. Toms are more assertive and often more aggressive than neutered males.

If they are allowed any outdoor freedom, they will become involved in battles with the local toms. Consequently, they will soon lose their handsome looks! Most cat breeders do not even keep males because of the problems and costs they entail. These cats are best kept in catteries where the owners have the time, the funds and everything else needed to justify their retention.

breeding females is a major commitment.

Before deciding whether breeding really is something you want to do, what would make good sense would be to neuter the pet and then become an exhibitor. When you have exhibited a number of times, your knowledge of cats will be greater, as will your contacts. You will be more aware of what quality is all about, and what it will cost for a well-bred female. It will be like an apprenticeship. Whether you then become a breeder, remain an exhibitor or prefer life as a pet owner, you will be glad you heeded the words of advice given here.

STOCK SELECTION

Stock selection revolves around health, quality, sex and age. Before these are discussed, it should be stated that many beginners unwisely rush this process. It is essential that ample time be devoted to researching from whom to purchase. This decision will influence a novice breeder's entire future endeavours.

HEALTH

Cats should only be obtained from a breeder whose stock has been tested negative for FeLV, FIP and FIV. The stock should be current on all vaccinations and worm treatments. Additionally, its blood type should be known so as to avoid incompatibility problems.

QUALITY

This must come in two forms. One is in the individual cat's appearance; the other is in its genetic ability to pass on the quality of its parents. The best way of obtaining these paired needs is to obtain initial stock from a breeder having a proven record of success with the Devon Rex, and with the colour you plan to start with. Being well acquainted with the breed's standard will be advantageous when seeking foundation stock. A female show cat attains her titles based on her appearance, but she may not pass on those looks to her offspring. Another cat that is very sound may pass on most of her good points and thus be more valuable for breeding. Of course, all litters will be influenced by the quality of the tom used. He will account for 50% of the offspring's genes. When viewing a litter of kittens, never forget that they are the result of the genes of two cats.

SEX

The beginner should only obtain females. The best advice is to commence with just one very sound female. By the time you have exhibited her and gained more knowledge about the finer points of the breed, you will be better able to judge what true

THE MALE STUD

The selection of a suitable stud should have been planned months before, as it can take some time to find the best male to use. It is preferred that the breeding lines of the stud are compatible with those of the female, meaning both pedigrees will carry a number of the same individuals in them. This is termed line-breeding. The ideal male will excel in those features that are considered weak in the female. You may read in other books that if a female is weak in a given feature, the ideal stud will be the total opposite. However, this can be misleading.

If the female has an overly long tail, what you do not need is a stud with a short tail. Rather, his tail should be as near the ideal length as possible. Genetically, this will improve tail length in your line without introducing unwanted genetic variance in your stock. Compensatory matings, such as short tail to long tail, will create such a variance. Once a male has been selected, ensure all his papers and vaccinations are in order. The female will be taken to the stud and left with him for a few days.

The odd-eyed
tortie tabby is
among the most
popular patterns
in the Devon Rex
breed.

THE BREEDING QUEEN

A female used for breeding purposes is called a queen. The principal requirement of such a cat is that she is an excellent example of the breed. This does not mean she must be a show winner. Many a winning exhibition cat has proved to have little breeding value. This is because a show cat gains success purely on its appearance; however, it may not pass those looks to its offspring.

A good breeding female may lack that extra something needed to be a top winner. Yet, she may pass on most of her excellent features to her offspring. Much will depend on the breeding line from which she was produced. Therefore any potential breeder must research existing breeders to ascertain which have good track records of producing consistently high-quality cats. In truth, and sadly, few newcomers in their haste to become breeders make this extra effort. This can result in becoming disillusioned if the female produces only average to inferior kittens.

WHAT'S A PEDIGREE WORTH?

When choosing breeding stock, never be dazzled by a pedigree. No matter how illustrious this is, it is only ever as good as the cat that bears it. If the cat is mediocre, then its prestigious pedigree is worthless from a breeding perspective. There are many other pitfalls for the novice when judging the value of a breeding line. These you must research in larger, more specialised books.

quality is all about. By then you will also have made many contacts on the show circuit. Alternatively, you may decide breeding is not for you and will have invested the minimum of time and money. A male is not needed until a breeder has become established. Even then, owning one is not essential to success. There is no shortage of quality studs. Males create many problems that the novice can do without. Once experience is gained, the new breeder can decide if owning a male would be of any particular benefit.

AGE

There is no specific age at which stock should be purchased but the following are suggested:
1. Most people purchase young kittens so they can enjoy them.

Breeding the Devon Rex is more challenging than with most other breeds, due to the complicated genetics involved. Producing a cat as stunning as this silver tortie tabby takes years of experience and dedication.

However, with such youngsters, their ultimate quality is harder to assess.

2. Chances are improved if a kitten has already won awards in shows. This will be when she is 14 weeks to 9 months of age, but she will be more costly.

3. A quality young female that has already produced offspring is a prudent choice but will be the most expensive option.

THE BREEDING PROCESS

Sexual maturity in cats may come as early as four months of age. Breeding should not be considered until the female is at least 12 months old, especially in the slow-maturing breeds such as those of Persian and European stock ancestry. A young cat barely out of her kitten stage may not have the required physical or psychological stability to produce and raise a vigorous litter. After her first heat, a female will normally come into heat again every two to three weeks and continue to do so until mated. The actual oestrous period lasts three to eight days. It is during this time that she is receptive to a male.

Once the mating has been successful, the time between fertilisation and birth of the young, known as the gestation period, is in the range of 59 to 67 days, 63 or 64 days being typical. The litter size will generally be

CAVEAT EMPTOR
When purchasing a kitten for breeding, make certain that the seller knows what your intentions are. If a kitten is registered on the non-active register, this means it was not considered by its breeder to be good enough for breeding. Any kittens bred from such a cat cannot be registered. You should also check that the mother of the kitten/young adult you are interested in has tested negative for feline leukaemia and that all other vaccinations are current.

two to five. Kittens are born blind and helpless, but develop rapidly. Their eyes open about the 10th-14th day. By 21 days, they start exploring. At this time they will also be sampling solid foods. By eight weeks, they can be vaccinated and neutered if required. Weaning normally commences by the age of six weeks and is completed within two to three weeks. Kittens can go

CAT CALLS
Females left in a non-spayed state are far more at risk from diseases and infections of the uterus. When in heat, the female becomes unusually affectionate and provocative. Her calls, a sound once heard never forgotten, can become extremely annoying if she is left unmated.

to a new home when 12 weeks old, though 14 to 16 weeks of age is preferred. During this period you must decide if you wish to register the kittens or merely 'declare' them. This allows them to be registered at a later time. Obtain the necessary information and forms from your cat-registration authority. You should also consider the benefits of registering your own breeder prefix. This, however, is only worthwhile if you intend to breed on a more than casual basis. If you have decided that certain kittens are unsuitable for showing/breeding, do consider early neutering.

NEWBORN KITTENS
Most kittens are born with body hair. Their ears and eyes, however, remain closed for about two weeks, though some ears and eyes become functional after 72 hours. Kittens should be allowed to nurse for seven weeks, longer if they will not readily eat and drink from a plate. If allowed to nurse, most kittens will stay on their mother's milk for two months or more.

Show-quality kittens are difficult to acquire. Considerable research and networking will be required to locate a top-bred Devon Rex kitten.

Coloration in the
Devon breed can
be overwhelming,
as there are so
many eye-catching
possibilities.
Consider these
two lovely colours:
a red-tipped
and a tortie.

Exhibiting Your
DEVON REX CAT

Without shows, the cat fancy could not exist. There would be only a handful of breeds as compared with today's ever-growing list. There would be fewer colour patterns and far less public awareness of cat welfare. Given the great importance of shows to the cat fancy, it is perhaps a little surprising, and disappointing, that the majority of cat owners have never visited a feline exhibition.

Shows such as the National and the Supreme of Britain, or their equivalents in other countries, are the shop windows of the world of domestic cats. They are meeting places where breeders from all over the country compete to establish how well their breeding programmes are developing. A show is also a major social event on the cat calendar.

Whether a potential pet owner or breeder of the future, you should visit one or two shows. It is a great day out for the whole family. Apart from the wonderful selection of breeds, there are also many trade stands. If a cat-related product is available, it will be

EXAMPLES OF CLASSES AT SHOWS

Open	Any cat of the specified breed.
Novice	Cats that have never won a first prize.
Limit	Cats that have not won more than first prizes.
Junior	Cats over nine months of age but less than two years on the day of the show.
Senior	Cats over two years old.
Visitors	Cats living a given distance away from the show venue.
Assessment	Experimental breeds that have an approved standard.
Aristocrat	Cats with one or two Challenge Certificates (or Premiers for neuters) so are not yet full Champions/Premiers.

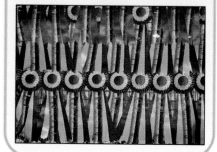

seen at the large exhibitions.

Many of the national clubs and magazines have stands. The two major shows mentioned are held in the winter months, usually November and December. However, there are hundreds of other shows staged during the year in various parts of the country. They range from small local club events to major championship breed shows and are usually advertised in the cat magazines. Your ruling cat association can also supply a list of shows.

SHOW ORGANISATION

So you will have some idea of how things are organised, the following information will be helpful. You will learn even more by purchasing the show catalogue. This contains the names and addresses of the exhibitors and details of their cats. It also lists the prizes, indicates the show regulations and carries many interesting advertisements.

A major show revolves around three broad categories of cats:
1. Unaltered cats, meaning those that are capable of breeding.
2. Neuters.
3. Non-pedigreed cats.

There is, thus, the opportunity for every type of cat, from the best Devon Rex to the everyday 'moggie,' to take part.

CLASSES FOR NON-PEDIGREED CATS

For non-pedigreed cats there are many classes, which include those for single colours, bicolours, tabbies, half-pedigreed, and so on. In this section are many delightful classes, such as those for cats owned by senior citizens, by young children (by age group), best original stray or rescued cat, best personality, most unusual looking, most photogenic and best older cat. Within this cat section can be seen some truly gorgeous felines. There is no doubt that the pet classes have been the springboard that has launched many a top breeder into the world of pedigreed cats.

These three broad categories are divided into various sections. For example, the unaltered and neuters are divided into their respective sections, such as Longhair, Semi-Longhair, British, Foreign, Siamese and so on.

There are many more classes other than those mentioned. These include club classes and those for kittens and non-pedigreed cats.

JUDGING

There are two ways cats can be judged. One is pen judging, the

BECOMING AN EXHIBITOR

Before any hobbyist enters a show, he is advised to join a local cat club. Here, hobbyists will meet local breeders who will not only assess their cats for them but also provide help on many other topics. The novice exhibitor could attend one or two shows with an exhibitor in order to learn the ropes. During this period, he can become familiar with the show rules and regulations. These are quite extensive, intended to safeguard the best interests of the hobby, the exhibitors and, most importantly, the cats.

It is of interest to note that some breeders own cats in partnership with other fanciers. This is useful when one person enjoys the breeding and the other the exhibition side. It enables both to really be involved in the hobby to a level that might not have been possible for either on his own. So, whether you fancy being an exhibitor or just love cats, do make a point of visiting the next major show in your area.

wins. In bench judging, stewards take the cats to the judge.

If a cat wins its class, it then competes against other class winners. By this process of elimination, a cat may go on to win the Best of Breed award. It then competes against other breed winners for the Best in Group award. The group winners compete for the Best in Show award.

A breeder can gather a number of awards during the course of a show. Even those who do not own the very best cats can take pride in gaining second, third, fourth and recommended, especially if won

ON THE CONTINENT AND BEYOND...

In Britain, the title of UK Grand Champion or Premier is won in competition with other Grand titleholders. In mainland Europe, cats can become International Champions. More British cats are expected to become International Champions with the recent introduction of passports for cats, allowing cats to compete more freely on the Continent and beyond. In countries other than Britain, the way in which shows are organised and titles achieved do differ somewhat. However, they broadly follow the outline discussed here.

other is bench or ring judging. In Britain, pen judging is the normal method, though bench judging is used for Best in Show. In pen judging, the judge moves around the cat pens. The cat gaining the most points when compared to the standard

Only Devon Rex cats that have won championships in the show ring should be considered for breeding purposes. The show ring is the proving ground for future generations of pure-bred cats.

at the larger shows. By progression, the top cat at a show will win its class, its breed, its section, and ultimately become the Best in Show exhibit. The titles a cat can win commence with that of Champion or Premier in the case of neuters. A Grand Champion, is made after winning in competition with others of its same status. The same applies to a Grand Premier. The judging system may vary from one country to another but the basis remains as outlined.

THE SHOW CAT

When a cat is seen preening in its pen, the hard work that has gone into its preparation is rarely appreciated. Exhibits must be in peak condition and their coats in top condition. The potential exhibit must be gradually trained to spend hours within its show pen. It must display no fear or aggression towards strangers, such as the stewards or the judges. These must be able to physically examine it, including its ears and teeth; it also involves being lifted into the air. If a cat scratches or bites a judge, or any other show official, it is automatically withdrawn from the show. A repeat of this in the future would result, in most instances, in the cat's show career being terminated by the ruling association.

Apart from being comfortable with people peering into its pen, the cat must be able to

Showing your
Devon Rex can be
rewarding,
though it is both
expensive and
time-consuming.
Only consider
showing if you
have a truly
top-quality
Devon Rex.

endure potentially long journeys to the show venue. Unless trained, the cat may become a nervous, aggressive feline that will have a very short show career.

Obviously, the cat must display quality. This means having none of the major faults that would prevent it from gaining a first prize. These are listed in the breed standard. The meaning of quality is very subjective. You do not need to own a potential champion to be a successful exhibitor. The cat must also be registered with the association under whose rules the show is being run. In Britain, this will be the Governing Council of the Cat Fancy (GCCF) or The Cat Association of Britain.

As in any competitive event, exhibits can gain prizes at the lower levels of a hobby without having any realistic chance of awards in the major shows. Owning such exhibits is often part of a top breeder-exhibitor's portfolio from their early days in the hobby. Others may never move beyond the smaller shows but still gain reputations for owning sound stock. They thoroughly enjoy being involved at their given level.

If the idea of exhibiting appeals to you, the best way to make a start is to join a local club. There you not only will be advised on all procedures but also will be able to make many new friends. Exhibiting can be costly in cash and time, but you can focus on the more local shows and attend the larger ones as a visitor.

'VETTING IN'

In England, cats are examined by a veterinary surgeon upon arrival to a show to make sure that they appear healthy. This process is called 'vetting in.' If the cat is rejected, it cannot be exhibited again until it receives a 'clearance certificate.' The possible reasons for rejection are stated in the rule book, which can be obtained at the show.

Health Care of Your
DEVON REX CAT

Maintaining a cat in the peak of good health revolves around the implementation of a sound

A LONG, HEALTHY LIFE

As veterinary surgeons make medical advances in the health care of cats, the longevity of the typical house cat is improving. Certainly ages between 15 and 18 years are not uncommon, and reports of cats living more than 20 years are predictable.

husbandry strategy. At the basic level, this means being responsible about feeding, cleanliness, and grooming. However, in spite of an owner's best efforts in these matters, cats may still become ill due to other causes. Although owners can attempt to prevent, identify and react to problems, only a vet is qualified to diagnose and suggest and/or effect remedies. Attempts by owners or 'informed' friends to diagnose and treat for specific diseases are dangerous and potentially life-threatening to the cat.

SELECTING A VETERINARY SURGEON

Your selection of a veterinary surgeon should not be based upon personality (as most are) but upon convenience to your home. You want a vet who is close because you might have emergencies or need to make multiple visits for treatments. You want a vet who has services that you might require such as nail clipping and bathing, as well as knowledge of recent medical findings and treatments and a good reputation for ability and responsiveness.

HEALTHY CAT

The enormous population of pet cats has stimulated the veterinary medical community to learn more about cats and to develop more modern medicines to keep felines healthier.

A DELICATE HEART

A cat's heart is as delicate as a human's heart, but it is much smaller. At full maturity, a queen's heart weighs between 9–12 grammes. The tom's heart is heavier, weighing 11–18 grammes. The blood that circulates through the heart chambers does not supply the heart muscle, thus requiring a separate circulatory system for the heart muscle.

There is nothing more frustrating than having to wait a day or more to get a response from your veterinary surgeon.

All veterinary surgeons are licensed and their diplomas and/or certificates should be displayed in their waiting rooms. There are, however, many veterinary specialities that usually require further studies and internships. There are specialists in heart problems (veterinary cardiologists), skin problems (veterinary dermatologists), teeth and gum problems (veterinary dentists), eye problems (veterinary ophthalmologists) and x-rays (veterinary radiologists), as well as vets who have specialities in reproduction, nutrition and behaviour. Eye disease is an area of increasing concern to all cat owners. Most veterinary surgeons do routine surgery, such as neutering and stitching up wounds. When the problem affecting your cat is serious, it is not unusual or impudent to get another medical opinion, although in Britain you are obliged to advise the vets concerned about this. You might also want to compare costs among several veterinary surgeons. Sophisticated health care and veterinary services can be very costly. It is not infrequent that important decisions are based upon financial considerations.

THE RIB CAGE

Cats usually have 13 pairs of ribs. The ribs in the middle are longer than the ribs on either end (or beginning) of the rib cage. The first nine ribs are joined to the chest bone (sternum) with costal cartilages. Ribs 10, 11 and 12 are also associated with cartilage, which contributes to the costal arch. The thirteenth rib is called the floating rib and its cartilage is separate from the other ribs.

PREVENTATIVE MEDICINE

It is much easier, less costly and more effective to practise preventative medicine than to fight bouts of illness and disease. Properly

KEEPING YOUR CAT HEALTHY

Although there are a multitude of ailments, diseases and accidents that could befall a cat, all but the most minor of problems can be avoided with good management. The following tips are a recipe for keeping your cat in the peak of health.

- Make sure it is vaccinated and in other ways protected from each of the major diseases. It must also receive annual boosters to maintain immunity.
- Have periodic checks made by your vet to see if your cat has worms.
- Ensure the cat receives an adequate diet that is both appealing and balanced.
- Have the kitten neutered if it is not to be used for breeding.
- Ensure the cat's litter tray, food/water vessels and grooming tools are always maintained in spotless condition.
- Do not let your cat out overnight or when you are away working or shopping.
- Always wash your hands after gardening or petting other people's pets.
- Groom your cat regularly. If this is done, you will more readily notice fleas or other problems than if grooming was done infrequently.
- Never try to diagnose and treat problems that are clearly of an internal type. Remember, even the most informed of breeders is not a vet and unable to reliably diagnose problems for you or advise treatments. Contact your vet.
- If you are ever in doubt about the health of your cat, do not delay in discussing your concerns with your vet. Delays merely allow problems to become more established.

bred kittens come from parents who were selected based upon their genetic-disease profile. Their mothers should have been vaccinated, free of all internal and external parasites and properly nourished. For these reasons, a visit to the veterinary surgeon who cared for the queen is recommended. The queen can pass on disease resistance to her kittens, which can last for eight to ten weeks. She can also pass on parasites and many infections. That's why you should visit the veterinary surgeon who cared for the queen.

VACCINATIONS

Most vaccinations are given by injection and should only be done by a veterinary surgeon. Both he and you should keep a record of the date of the injection, the identification of the vaccine and the amount given. The first vaccination is normally given when the kitten is about 8–9 weeks old. About 30 days later, a booster is given. Although there are many diseases to which a cat may fall victim, the most dangerous three—FIE, FVR and FeLV—can be safeguarded against with a single (three-in-one)

BLOOD GROUP INCOMPATIBILITY (BGI)

In recent years, blood group incompatibility has become the focus of scientists, vets and breeders. Its importance to pet owners is when transfusions are needed. For breeders, it probably accounts for a large percentage of kittens that die from fading kitten syndrome. Scientifically the problem is called neonatal erythrolysis, meaning the destruction of red blood cells in newly born offspring.

Cats have two blood groups, A & B. Group A is dominant to B (which is genetically called recessive). When the antibodies of B-group mothers are passed to A-group kittens, via her colostrum milk, they destroy red blood cells. Death normally follows within a few days.

Most domestic cats tested are group A. However, national and regional differences display a variation in which 1-6% may be of type B. In pedigreed breeds, it has been found that the number of group-B cats varies significantly. The following breeds, based on present available data, have the indicated percentage incidence of group-B blood type.

0%	Siamese, Burmese and Oriental Shorthair
1-5%	Maine Coon, Manx and Norwegian Forest
10-20%	Abyssinian, Birman, Japanese Bobtail, Persian, Scottish Fold and Somali
25-50%	Devon and Cornish Rex, British Shorthair and Exotic Shorthair

The clear implication to breeders is to establish their cats' blood group, via testing, and conduct appropriate matings. These should not result in B-group mothers' nursing A-group kittens.

The safe matings are:

1. Group-A males   x   A females
2. Group-B males   x   A or B females
3. Group-A females x   A or B males
4. Group-B females x   B males

Breeders are advised to seek further information before embarking on stock purchase and breeding programmes.

injection. Thereafter, an annual booster is all that is required.

MAJOR DISEASES

There are a number of diseases for which there is either no cure or little chance of recovery. However, some can be prevented by vaccination. All breeders and owners should ensure kittens are so protected.

FELINE INFECTIOUS ENTERITIS (FIE)

This is known variously as feline panleukopenia, feline distemper and feline parvovirus. The virus attacks the intestinal system. It is spread via the faeces and urine. The virus may survive for many years in some environments. The use of household bleach (sodium hypochlorite) for cleaning helps to prevent colonisation. Signs, among others, are diarrhoea, vomiting, depression, anorexia and dehydration. Death may occur within days. A vaccine is available from your vet.

FELINE VIRAL RHINOTRACHEITIS (FVR) & CALCIVIRUS (FCV)

Also known as cat flu, this is a complex of upper respiratory diseases. Signs are excessive hard sneezing, runny nose and mouth ulcers. Cats vaccinated after having contracted flu may recover but may suffer recurrent bouts, especially if they become stressed.

HEALTH AND VACCINATION SCHEDULE

AGE	6 WKS	8 WKS	10 WKS	12 WKS	16 WKS	6 MOS	1 YR
Worm control	✔	✔	✔		✔		
Neutering						✔	
Rhinotracheitis	✔	✔		✔	✔		✔
Panleukopenia	✔	✔		✔			✔
Calcivirus		✔			✔		✔
Feline Leukaemia				✔			✔
Feline Infectious Peritonitis				✔	✔		✔
Faecal evaluation						✔	
Feline Immunodeficiency testing							✔
Feline Leukaemia testing				✔			✔
Dental evaluation		✔				✔	
Rabies				✔	✔		✔

Vaccinations are not instantly effective. It takes about two weeks for the cat's immune system to develop antibodies. Most vaccinations require annual booster shots. Your veterinary surgeon should guide you in this regard.

DISEASE REFERENCE CHART

	What is it?	Cause	Symptoms
Feline Leukaemia Virus (FeLV)	Infectious disease; kills more cats each year than any other feline infectious disease.	A virus spread through saliva, tears, urine and faeces of infected cats; bite wounds.	Early on no symptoms may occur, but eventually infected cats experience signs from depression and weight loss to respiratory distress. FeLV also suppresses immune system, making a cat susceptible to almost any severe chronic illness.
Rabies	Potentially deadly virus that infects warm-blooded mammals.	A bacterium, often carried by rodents, that enters through mucous membranes and spreads quickly throughout the body.	Aggressiveness, a blank or vacant look in the eyes, increased vocalisation and/or weak or wobbly gait.
Feline Infectious Enteritis (FIE) *aka Panleukopenia*	Highly contagious virus, potentially deadly.	Ingestion of the virus, which is usually spread through the faeces of infected cats.	Most common: severe diarrhoea. Also vomiting, fatigue, lack of appetite, severe inflammation of intestines.
Feline Viral Rhinotracheitis (FVR)	Viral disease that affects eyes and upper respiratory tracts.	A virus that can affect any cat, especially those in multiple-cat settings.	Sneezing attacks, coughing, drooling thick saliva, fever, watery eyes, ulcers of mouth, nose and eyes.
Feline Immuno-deficiency Virus (FIV)	Virus that reduces white blood cells.	An infection spread commonly through cat-fight wounds.	Signs may be dormant for years or innocuous, such as diarrhoea or anaemia.
Feline Infectious Peritonitis (FIP)	A fatal viral disease, may be linked to FeLV and FIV.	Bacteria in dirty litter boxes; stress may increase susceptibility in kittens.	Extremely variable; range from abdominal swelling to chest problems, eye ailments and body lesions.
Feline Urological Syndrome (FUS)	A disease that affects the urinary tracts of cats.	Inflammation of bladder and urethra.	Constipation, constant licking of penis or vulva, blood in urine (males), swollen abdomen, crying when lifted.

CLEANLINESS IS THE KEY

Crucial to the prevention and spread of disease is the need to maintain meticulous cleanliness, especially relating to the litter tray. Many diseases and problems are transferred via faecal matter. Once a problem is suspected, the advice of a vet should be sought. Blood tests, faecal microscopy and other testing methods are now available. They can mean the difference between life and death of a cherished pet.

FELINE LEUKAEMIA VIRUS (FELV)

This is an highly infectious viral disease. It is spread via direct contact—mutual grooming, saliva, feeding bowls, faeces, urine and biting. It can be passed prenatally from a female to her offspring. It creates tumours, anaemia, immune system depression, pyrexia (high temperatures), lethargy, respiratory disease, intestinal disease and many other potentially fatal problems. It is most prevalent in high-density cat populations. Not all cats will be affected, but they may become carriers.

Kittens less than six months old are especially vulnerable. Infected cats usually die by the time they are three to four years old. Cats can be screened or tested for this disease. Vaccination is not 100% effective but is recommended in kittens being sold into multi-cat environments.

FELINE IMMUNODEFICIENCY VIRUS (FIV)

This causes the white blood cells to be significantly reduced, thus greatly suppressing the efficiency of the immune system. It is not transferable to humans. Infection is normally gained from cat-fight wounds; thus, outdoor males are at the most risk. A cat diagnosed via blood tests as FIV-positive may live a normal life for months or years if retained indoors and given careful attention. Signs may be innocuous in the early stages, such as anaemia or diarrhoea. No vaccine is available.

FELINE INFECTIOUS PERITONITIS (FIP)

This viral disease is invariably fatal once contracted in its more potent forms. However, the virulence of the virus is variable and may by destroyed by the immune system. Stress may increase susceptibility in kittens. It may be linked to FeLV and FIV. Signs are extremely variable and range from abdominal swelling to chest problems, eye ailments to body lesions. There are various tests available but none is as yet 100% conclusive. Strict cleanliness is essential, especially of litter trays. No vaccine is available.

FELINE UROLOGICAL SYNDROME (FUS)

This is a very distressing condition caused by an inflammation of the bladder and urethra. Signs are constipation-like squatting and attempts to urinate, regular licking of the penis or vulva, blood in urine (males), swollen abdomen, crying when lifted and urinating in unusual places (often in only small amounts).

The numerous causes include infection, dirty litter tray of the indoor cat, alkaline urine (in cats it should be acidic), diet too dry, poor water intake (even though this may be available) and being hit by a vehicle (damaged nerves).

CARE OF FELINE KIDNEYS

The kidney of the cat is larger than that of the dog, but it has the typical bean shape. It receives 25% of the blood output of the heart! For this reason, it has rather significant veins to accommodate this large supply of blood, and injuries suffered by the kidneys are usually serious and not uncommon.

NEUTERING

Neutering is a major means of avoiding ill health. It dramatically reduces the risk of males' becoming involved in territorial battles with the dangers of physical injury and disease transference. It makes the male more placid and less likely to scent mark its home. It also reduces the incidence of prostate problems, and there is no risk of testicular cancer. The female avoids potentially lethal illnesses related to her being allowed to remain in an unmated condition, such as breast cancer.

Neutering is usually performed between four and six months of age, but it can be done as early as eight weeks of age. Data available on the age at which a kitten is neutered indicate that early neutering has more advantages than drawbacks. Breeders should have this performed on all cats sold as pets.

Male cats are neutered. The operation removes the testicles and requires that the cat be anaesthetised. Females are spayed. This is major surgery during which the ovaries and uterus are removed. Both males and females should be kept quiet at home for about seven to ten days following the procedure, at which time the vet will remove the sutures.

Veterinary treatment is essential or the condition could be fatal due to the bladder's bursting or the presence of dangerous bacteria.

RABIES

Currently, Britain and most European Community countries are free of this terrible disease. The quarantine laws of Britain are such that vaccination has not been necessary. However, the introduction of passports for dogs and cats means that resident British cats must be vaccinated if they are to travel abroad and return to the UK without being placed into quarantine. The vaccination is given when the kitten is three or more months old. The pet passport process takes at least six months to complete, so plan well ahead.

COMMON HEALTH PROBLEMS

DERMATITIS (ECZEMA)

Dry, lifeless coat, loss of coat, tiny scabs over the head and body, loose flakes (dandruff) and excessive scratching are all commonly called eczema. The cause covers a range of possibilities including diet, parasitic mites such as *Cheyletiella spp*, fungus or an allergy to flea or other bites. Sometimes reasons are unknown. Veterinary diagnosis and treatment are required.

RINGWORM (*DERMATOPHYTOSIS*)

This problem is fungal, not that of a worm. The most common form is *Microsporum canis*,

POSSIBLE SOURCES OF EAR PROBLEMS

- Fight scratches
- Excess secretion of wax
- Swellings and blood blisters (haematoma) resulting from intrusion by foreign bodies (grass seeds, etc.)
- Sunburn
- Whitish-coloured ear mites (*Otodectes cynotis*)
- Orange-coloured harvest mites (*Trombicula autumnalis*)
- Fleas
- Bacterial infection of either the outer or middle/inner ear

type bald areas of skin, which may be flaked and reddish. The coat generally may become dry and lifeless, giving the appearance of numerous other skin and hair problems. Veterinary diagnosis and treatment, either topical or via drugs, are essential as the condition is zoonotic, meaning that it can be transferred to humans.

EAR PROBLEMS

Most of the common ear problems affect the outer ear. The telltale sign is the cat's constant scratching of the ears and/or its holding the ear to one side. Greasy hairs around the ear, dark brown wax (cerumen) in the ears, scaly flakes in or around the ear or minute white or orange pinhead-like bodies (mites) in the ear are common signs. Canker is a term used for ear infections, but it has no specific meaning.

Over-the-counter remedies for ear problems are usually ineffective unless correct diagnosis has been made. It is therefore better to let the vet diagnose and treat the cat. Some problems may require anaesthesia and minor surgery.

DIARRHOEA

This is a general term used to indicate a semi-liquid to liquid state of faecal matter. Mild to acute cases may be due to a

which accounts for over 90% of cases. Cats less than one year old are at the highest risk, while longhaired cats are more prone to the problem than shorthaired cats. The fungi feed on the keratin layers of the skin, nails and hair. Direct contact and spores that remain in the environment are the main means of transmission.

Typical signs are circular-

change of environment, dietary change, eating an 'off' item, gorging on a favoured food, stress or a minor chill. These often rectify themselves within days. Chronic and persistent diarrhoea may be the result of a specific disease. Any indication of blood in the faecal matter must be considered dangerous.

In minor cases, withholding food for 12–24 hours, or feeding a simple diet, may arrest the condition. If not, contact your vet. Faecal analysis and blood testing may be required. By asking numerous questions related to the cat's diet, general health, level of activity, loss of appetite, etc., the vet can determine whether tests are required or if immediate treatment is warranted. Do not give cats human or canine intestinal remedies; these could prove dangerous.

CONSTIPATION

A cat's straining and inability to pass motions are indicative of various causes. It may have hairballs, may have eaten a bird or rodent and has a bone lodged in its intestinal tract, may be suffering from a urological problem rather than constipation, or may have been hit by a car and has damaged the nerves that control bowel movements. As constipation is potentially serious, veterinary advice should be sought. Laxatives and faecal softener tablets may be given, the faecal matter can be surgically removed or another treatment carried out.

If your Devon Rex is acting strangely, by avoiding contact, hiding or moping around the home, it may not be feeling well. Any sudden change in behaviour should be reported to your vet.

EXTERNAL PARASITES

FLEAS

Of all the problems to which cats are prone, none is more well known and frustrating than fleas. Indeed, flea-related problems are the principal cause of visits to veterinary surgeons. Flea infestation is relatively simple to cure but difficult to prevent. Periodic flea checks for your cat, conducted as well as annual health check-ups, are highly recommended. Consistent dosing with anthelmintic preparations is also advised. Parasites that are harboured inside the body are a bit more difficult to eradicate, but they are easier to control.

To control a flea infestation, you have to understand the flea's life cycle. Fleas are often thought of as a summertime problem but centrally heated homes have changed the life-cycle patterns, and fleas can be found at any time of the year. Fleas thrive in hot and humid environments; they soon die if the temperature drops below 2°C (35°F). The most effective method of flea control is a two-stage approach: one stage to kill the adult fleas, and the other to control the development of pre-adult fleas. Unfortunately, no single active ingredient is effective against all stages of the life cycle.

Flea prevention is a challenge to cat owners in most places. This is an adult male flea.

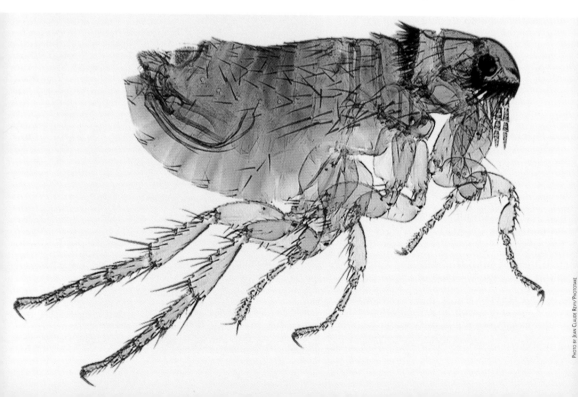

PHOTO BY JEAN CLAUDE REVY/PHOTOTAKE

A Look at Fleas

Fleas have been around for millions of years and have adapted to changing host animals. They are able to go through a complete life cycle in less than one month, or they can extend their lives to almost two years by remaining as pupae or cocoons. They must have a blood meal every 10-14 days, and egg production begins within 2 days of their first meal. The female cat flea is very prolific and can lay 2000 eggs in her lifetime!

Fleas have been measured as being able to jump 300,000 times and can jump 150 times their body length in any direction, including straight up. Those are just a few of the reasons why they are so successful in infesting a cat!

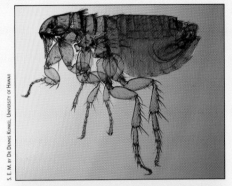

A scanning electron micrograph (S. E. M.) of a flea.

Magnified head of a flea.

LIFE CYCLE STAGES

During its life, a flea will pass through four life stages: egg, larva, pupa and adult. The adult stage is the most visible and irritating stage of the flea life cycle, and this is why the majority of flea-control products concentrate on this stage. The fact is that adult fleas account for only 1% of the total flea population, and the other 99% exist in pre-adult stages, i.e. eggs, larvae and pupae. The pre-adult stages are barely visible to the naked eye.

THE LIFE CYCLE OF THE FLEA

Eggs are laid on the cat, usually in quantities of about 20 or 30, several times a day. The female adult flea must have a blood meal before each egg-laying session. When first laid, the eggs will not cling to the cat's fur, as the eggs are not sticky. They will immediately fall to the floor or ground, especially when the cat moves around or scratches.

Once the eggs fall from the cat onto the carpet or grass, they will hatch into yellow larvae, approximately 2 mms long. This takes from 5 to 11 days. Larvae are not particularly mobile and will usually travel only a few inches from where they hatch. However, they do have a tendency to move away from light and heavy traffic—under furniture, in the carpet and behind doors are common places to find high quantities of flea larvae.

The flea larvae feed on dead organic matter, including adult flea faeces, until they are ready to change into adult fleas. Fleas will usually remain as larvae for around seven days, becoming darker in colour. After this period, the larvae will pupate a protective cocoon. While inside the pupae, the larvae will undergo metamorphosis and change into adult fleas. This can happen within a week, but the adult fleas can remain inside the pupae waiting to hatch for up to six months. The pupae are signalled to hatch by certain stimuli, such as physical pressure—the pupae's being stepped on, heat from an animal lying on the pupae or increased

Opposite page: A scanning electron micrograph of a flea, magnified more than 100x. This image has been colorized for effect.

DID YOU KNOW?
Flea-killers are poisonous. You should not spray these toxic chemicals on areas of a cat's body that he licks, on his genitals or on his face. Flea killers taken internally are a better answer, but check with your vet in case internal therapy is not advised for your cat.

carbon dioxide levels and vibrations—indicating that a suitable host is available.

Once hatched, the adult flea must feed within a few days. Once the adult flea finds a host, it will not leave voluntarily. It only becomes dislodged by grooming or the host animal's scratching. The adult flea will remain on the host for the duration of its life unless forcibly removed.

TREATING THE ENVIRONMENT AND THE CAT
Treating fleas should be a two-pronged attack. First, the environment needs to be treated; this includes carpets and furniture, especially the cat's bedding and areas underneath furniture. The environment should be treated with a household spray containing an Insect Growth Regulator (IGR) and an insecticide to kill the adult fleas. There are also liquids, given orally, that contain chitin inhibitors. These

DID YOU KNOW?
Never mix flea-control products without first consulting your veterinary surgeon. Some products can become toxic when combined with others and can cause serious or fatal consequences.

A brown tick, *Rhipicephalus sanguineus*, is an uncommon but annoying tick found on cats.

render flea eggs incapable of development. There are also both foam and liquid wipe-on treatments. Additionally, cats can be injected with treatments that can last up to six months. Emulsions that have the same effect can also be added to food. The advanced treatments are only available from veterinary surgeons. The IGRs actually mimic the fleas' own hormones and stop the eggs and larvae from developing into adult fleas. There are currently no treatments available to attack the pupa stage of the life cycle, so the adult insecticide is used to kill the newly hatched adult fleas before they find a host. Most IGRs are active for many months, while adult insecticides are only active for a few days.

The head of a tick, *Dermacentor variabilis*, enlarged and coloured for effect.

When treating with a household spray, it is a good idea to vacuum before applying the product. This stimulates as many pupae as possible to hatch into adult fleas. The vacuum cleaner should also be treated with a flea

Dwight R Kuhn's magnificent action photo, showing a flea jumping.

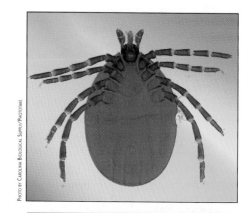

PHOTO BY CAROLINA BIOLOGICAL SUPPLY/PHOTOTAKE

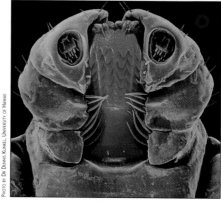

PHOTO BY DR DENNIS KUNKEL, UNIVERSITY OF HAWAII

treatment to prevent the eggs and larvae that have been hoovered into the vacuum bag from hatching.

The second stage of treatment is to apply an adult insecticide to the cat, usually in the form of a collar or a spray. Alternatively, there are drops that, when placed on the back of the animal's neck, spread throughout the fur and skin to kill adult fleas. A word of warning: Never use products sold for dogs on your cat; the result could be fatal.

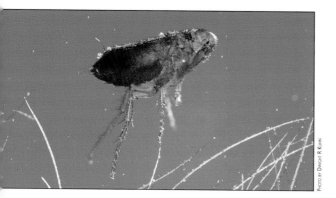

PHOTO BY DWIGHT R KUHN

The Life Cycle of the Flea

Eggs

Larvae

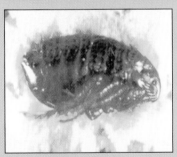

Pupa

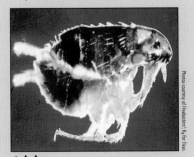

Adult

Photos courtesy of Fleabusters' Rx for Fleas.

Flea Control

IGR (INSECT GROWTH REGULATOR)

Two types of products should be used when treating fleas—a product to treat the pet and a product to treat the home. Adult fleas represent 1% of the flea population. The pre-adult fleas (eggs, larvae and pupae) represent 99% of the flea population and are found in the environment; it is in the case of pre-adult fleas that products containing an Insect Growth Regulator (IGR) should be used in the home.

IGRs are a new class of compounds used to prevent the development of insects. They do not kill the insect outright, but instead use the insect's biology against it to stop it from completing its growth. Products that contain methoprene are the world's first and leading IGRs. Used to control fleas and other insects, this type of IGR will stop flea larvae from developing and protect the house for up to seven months.

EN GARDE: CATCHING FLEAS OFF GUARD!

Consider the following ways to arm yourself against fleas:
• Add a small amount of pennyroyal or eucalyptus oil to your cat's bath. These natural remedies repel fleas.
• Supplement your cat's food with fresh garlic (minced or grated) and a hearty amount of brewer's yeast, both of which ward off fleas.
• Use a flea comb on your cat daily. Submerge fleas in a cup of bleach to kill them quickly.
• Confine the cat to only a few rooms to limit the spread of fleas in the home.
• Vacuum daily...and get all of the crevices! Dispose of the bag every few days until the problem is under control.
• Wash your cat's bedding daily. Cover cushions where your cat sleeps with towels, and wash the towels often.

Opposite page:
The tick
*Dermacentor
variabilis* is one
of the most
common ticks
found on cats.
Look at the
strength in its
eight legs! No
wonder it's hard
to detach them.

TICKS AND MITES

Though not as common as fleas, ticks and mites are found all over the tropical and temperate world. They don't bite like fleas; they harpoon. They dig their sharp proboscis (nose) into the cat's skin and drink the blood. Their only food and drink is your cat's blood. Cats can get potentially fatal anaemia, paralysis and many other diseases from ticks and mites. They may live where fleas are found and they like to hide in cracks or seams in walls wherever cats live. They are controlled the same way fleas are controlled.

The *Dermacentor variabilis* may well be the most common tick in many geographical areas, especially those areas where the climate is hot and humid. The other common ticks that attack small animals are *Rhipicephalus sanguineus, Ixodes* and some species of *Amblyomma.*

Most ticks have life expectancies of a week to six months, depending upon climatic conditions. They can neither jump nor fly, but they can crawl slowly and can range up to 5 metres (16 feet) to reach a sleeping or unsuspecting animal.

INTERNAL PARASITES

Most animals—fishes, birds and mammals, including cats and humans—have worms and other parasites that live inside their bodies. According to Dr Herbert R Axelrod, the fish pathologist, there are two kinds of parasites: dumb and smart. The smart parasites live in peaceful cooperation with their hosts (symbiosis), while the dumb parasites kill their hosts. Most of the worm infections are relatively

TOXOPLASMOSIS AND PREGNANT WOMEN

Toxoplasmosis is caused by a single parasite, *Toxoplasma gondii.* Cats acquire it by eating infected prey, such as rodents or birds, or raw meat. Obviously, strictly indoor cats are at less risk of infection than cats that are permitted to roam outdoors. Symptoms include diarrhoea, listlessness, pneumonia and inflammation of the eye. Sometimes there are no symptoms. The disease can be treated with antibiotics.

The only way humans can get the disease is through direct contact with the cat's faeces. People usually don't display any symptoms, although they can show mild flu-like symptoms. Once exposed, an antibody is produced and the person builds immunity to the disease.

The real danger to humans is that pregnant women can pass the parasite to the developing foetus. In this case, the chances are good that the baby will be born with a major health problem and/or serious birth defects. In order to eliminate risk, pregnant women should have someone else deal with the litter-box duties or wear gloves while taking care of the litter box and wash hands thoroughly afterwards.

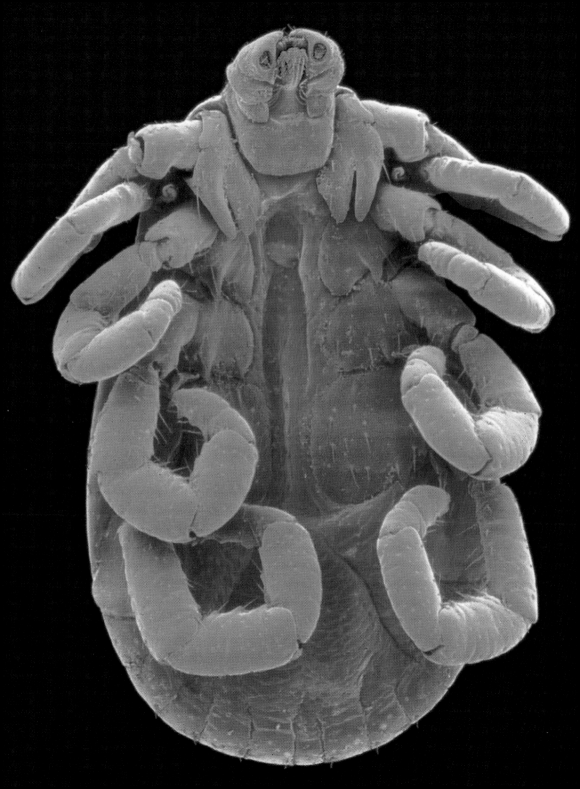

easy to control. If they are not controlled, they weaken the host cat to the point that other medical problems occur, but they are not dumb parasites.

HOOKWORMS

The worm *Ancylostoma tubaeforme* can infect a cat by larva penetrating its skin. It attaches itself to the small intestine of the cat, where it sucks blood. This loss of blood could cause iron-deficiency anaemia.

Outdoor cats that spend much of their time in the garden or in contact with soil are commonly infected with hookworm. There is another worm, the *Gordius* or horsehair worm, that, if ingested by a cat, causes vomiting.

TAPEWORMS

There are many species of tapeworms. They are carried by

DEWORMING
Ridding your kitten of worms is VERY IMPORTANT because certain worms that kittens carry, such as tapeworms and roundworms, can infect humans.

Breeders initiate a deworming programme at or about four weeks of age. The routine is repeated every two or three weeks until the kitten is three months old. The breeder from whom you obtained your kitten should provide you with the complete details of the deworming programme.

Your veterinary surgeon can prescribe and monitor the programme of deworming for you. The usual programme is treating the kitten every 15–20 days until the kitten is positively worm-free.

It is advised that you only treat your kitten with drugs that are recommended professionally.

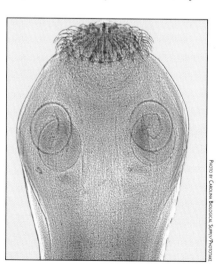

The head and rostellum (the round prominence on the scolex) of a tapeworm, which infects cats and humans.

PHOTO BY CAROLINA BIOLOGICAL SUPPLY/PHOTOTAKE

fleas! The cat eats the flea and starts the tapeworm cycle. Humans can also be infected with tapeworms, so don't eat fleas! Fleas are so small that your cat could pass them onto your hands, your plate or your food and thus make it possible for you to ingest a flea that is carrying tapeworm eggs.

While tapeworm infection is not life-threatening in cats (smart parasite!), it can be the cause of a

INTERNAL PARASITES OF CATS

NAME	DESCRIPTION	SYMPTOMS	ACQUISITION	TREATMENT
Roundworm (*Toxocara cati* and *Toxascaris leonina*)	Large, white, coil-like worms, 5–10 cms (2–4 inches) long, resembling small springs.	Vomiting, pot belly, respiratory problems, poor growth rate, protruding third eyelids, poor haircoat.	Ingesting infective larvae; ingesting infected mammals, birds or insects; a queen with *Toxocari cati* nursing kittens.	Anthelmintics; scrupulously clean environment (e.g. daily removal of all faeces recommended).
Physaloptera species	2–15 cms (1–6 inches) long, attacks the wall of the stomach.	Vomiting, anorexia, melena.	Eating insects that live in soil (e.g. May beetles).	Diagnosed with a gastroscope; treated with pyrantel pamoate. Prevention of exposure to the intermediate hosts.
Gordius or Horsehair worm	15-cms (6-inch) pale brown worms with stripes.	Vomiting.	May ingest a worm while drinking from or making contact with swimming pools and toilet bowls.	Anthelmintics; avoiding potentially infected environments.
Hookworm (*Ancylostoma tubaeforme*)	The adult worms, ranging from 6 to 15 mms (2.5–6 inches) in length, attach themselves to the small intestines.	Anaemia, melena, weight loss, poor haircoat.	Larva penetrating the cat's skin, usually attacks the small intestine. Found in soil and flower gardens where faecal matter is deposited.	Fortnightly treatment with anthelmintics. Good sanitation (e.g. daily cleanup of litter boxes).
Tapeworm (*Dipylidium caninum* and *Taenia taeniformis*)	Up to 91 cms (3 feet) long. Parts shaped similar to cucumber seeds. The most common intermediate hosts are fleas and biting lice.	No clinical signs—difficult to detect.	Eating infected adult fleas. Uses rodents as hosts.	Praziquantel and epsiprantel. Management of environment to ensure scrupulously clean conditions. Proper flea control.

Magnified heartworm larvae, *Dirofilaria immitis*.

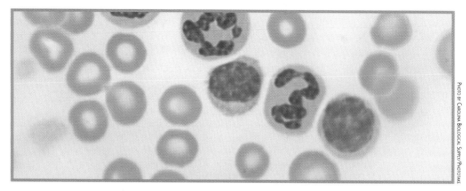

PHOTO BY CAROLINA BIOLOGICAL SUPPLY/PHOTOTAKE

The heartworm, *Dirofilaria immitis*.

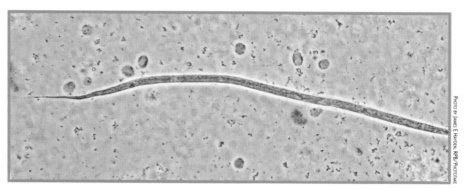

PHOTO BY JAMES E HAYDEN, RPB, PHOTOTAKE

very serious liver disease for humans. About 50 percent of the humans infected with *Echinococcus multilocularis*, a type of tapeworm that causes alveolar hydatis, perish.

HEARTWORMS

Heartworms are thin, extended worms up to 30 cms (12 ins) long, which are difficult to diagnose in cats as the worms are too few to be identified by the antigen-detection test. Symptoms may be loss of energy, loss of appetite, coughing, the development of a potbelly and anaemia. Heartworm infection in cats should be treated very seriously, as it is often fatal.

Heartworms are transmitted by mosquitoes. The mosquito drinks the blood of an infected cat and takes in larvae with the blood. It takes two to three weeks for the larvae to develop to the infective stage within the body of the mosquito. Cats are less frequently infected with heartworms than dogs are. Also, the parasite is more likely to attack the cat's brain or other organs rather than the heart. Cats should be treated at about six weeks of age, and maintained on a prophylactic dose given monthly.

THE FELINE EYE

by Lorraine Waters BvetNed, CertVOphthal, MRCVS

This part of the book aims to provide an owner's guide to feline ophthalmology, the study of eyes, which is an area of increasing concern for cat owners.

Eye diseases in the cat usually result from trauma, infection or neoplasia. Unlike the dog, the cat has few inherited eye conditions. Most of the conditions to be discussed are not amenable to first-aid measures or home remedies. Therefore, if you are at all worried about your cat's eyes, you should seek prompt veterinary attention.

Ocular pain is frequently associated with eye disease and can be recognised in your cat because it will show a combination of the following signs:

blinking, increased tear production, fear of light and rubbing at the eye. Some conditions result in loss of vision; a gradual loss of vision may go unnoticed, as the cat slowly adapts, but a sudden loss produces an obvious change in behaviour. Being blind may not be as bad as it sounds, as cats adapt and cope amazingly well in familiar surroundings.

To examine the eye properly, veterinary surgeons first use a bright light, which allows close examination of the lids, conjunctiva, cornea and iris. Following this, an ophthalmoscope can be used, in a darkened room, to give a magnified view. Then, by using the lenses within the ophthalmoscope, it is possible to focus on the structures further back in the eye, such as the lens, vitreous and retina.

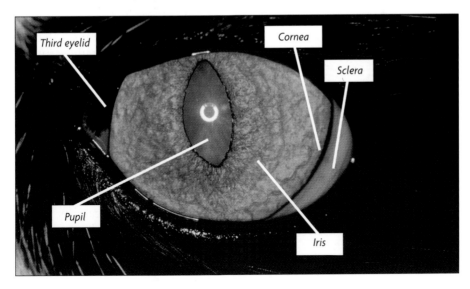

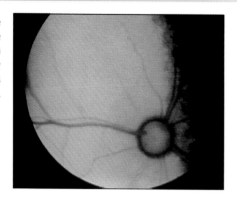

The feline fundus, the eye as seen through the veterinary surgeon's ophthalmoscope.

DISEASES OF THE FELINE EYE

GLOBE AND ORBIT

The eye sits in a bony socket in the skull known as the orbit. In short-nosed breeds, the orbit is shallow and the normal-sized eyes bulge forward. This situation can predis-pose a number of problems, such as exposure keratitis, overflow of tears and even prolapse of the globe (eye). Cats can be born with eyes that are too small and sink back into the orbit, to be covered by the third eyelid. This is non-inherited and usually associated with damage to the eye in utero. Abnormal enlargement of the globe may be congenital, buphthalmos, or acquired, hydrophthalmos, and is the end point of glaucoma.

The globe can prolapse from the orbit following head trauma, a common injury for cats involved in road traffic accidents. A minor prolapse replaced early can result in restoration of normal function. However, there is often stretching of the optic nerve and tearing of the extra-ocular muscles. In these cases, the eye may be permanently damaged and have to be surgically removed. As an emergency measure, applying a moist cloth to the prolapsed eye on the way to the surgery will help preserve it.

Problems behind the eye become evident when they cause the eye to bulge forward along with the third eyelid. These include tooth root abscesses, foreign bodies, tumours and occasionally haemorrhage.

EYELIDS

The eyes of a kitten should open around 10–14 days of age. Once this has occurred, it is possible to see if the lids have been properly formed. Failure of all or part of the eyelids to develop is a rare congen-ital problem, known as coloboma.

EYE DROPS

Topical ointments and drops are often prescribed for the treatment of eye disease. There are a few simple rules to follow when administering them. It is important to clean away discharges before applying treatment. Only give one drop or just a few millimetres of ointment; if you give too much it will be diluted by increased tear production. Systemic drugs are those given by mouth to achieve higher concentrations at the back of the eye or for diseases which involve other body systems.

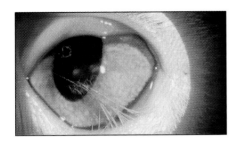

The unprotected cornea, in the affected area, may become damaged and the lid must be surgically restored. Early infection in the eye may delay or prevent eyelid opening; the lids can be opened surgically to allow bathing and appropriate medication to be given.

Entropion and ectropion are common conditions in the dog and are related to conformation. Fortunately these are rare in cats and can be surgically corrected. Entropion secondary to ocular pain may remain once the cause of the pain is removed. Fortunately these cases will respond to corrective surgery. Extra or abnormally positioned hairs are frequently seen as an inherited problem in dogs, but are rare in cats.

There are several types of tumours that can occur on the eyelids. The most common type is squamous cell carcinoma, more prevalent in white and part-white cats, as ultra-violet light (sunlight) plays a role in causing this condition. Treatment may consist of cryotherapy, surgical excision or radiation treatment. Early recogni-

tion and treatment are essential to prevent destructive local spreading.

CONJUNCTIVA
The pink tissue lining the eyelid and covering the third eyelid and front of the sclera is called conjunctiva. Dermoids are elements of skin tissue that arise in abnormal places. Dermoids often, but not invariably, contain hairs and can form on the conjunctiva and/or cornea. Dermoids act as foreign bodies in the eye, causing irritation and pain, and need to be surgically removed.

The most frequently encountered problem with the conjunctiva is conjunctivitis. In cats, the majority of cases are infectious. An eye with conjunctivitis usually looks red and swollen with signs of ocular pain. Discharges may be watery or sticky yellow, indicating bacterial infection.

The most common infectious cause of feline conjunctivitis is feline herpesvirus (FHV). Feline calicivirus (FCV) can also cause conjunctivitis and is usually associated with other signs, such as

Eyelid coloboma is a rare congenital problem in cats.

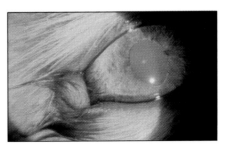

Dermoid in a longhaired cat.

Conjunctivitis, frequently an infectious disease in cats.

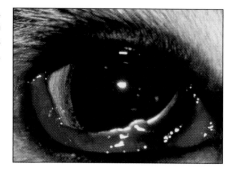

upper respiratory tract problems and mouth ulcers. The bacteria *Chlamydia psittaci* can cause conjunctivitis in individual cats and in multi-cat households.

Corneal ulcer stained with fluorescein.

Individual cases respond well to appropriate antibiotic therapy. Chronic and recurrent conjunctivitis in multi-cat situations requires thorough and prolonged treatment, management changes and, where appropriate, vaccination. *Mycoplasma spp.* can cause a less severe conjunctivitis than *Chlamydia spp.* Opportunistic infection can occur following cat-fight wounds, as bacteria are found on cats' teeth and claws.

Non-infectious causes of conjunctivitis include trauma,

Tear staining is more commonly seen in short-nosed cat breeds.

foreign bodies, allergic disease, tumours and pre-corneal tear film abnormalities. Eosinophilic kerato-conjunctivitis is a disease in which the conjunctiva and cornea are invaded by cells from the immune system, primarily mast cells and eosinophils. These cells are responsible for inflammation and allergic reactions. This tends to occur in young to middle-aged cats and may be seasonal. Treatment usually works well but may be required long-term.

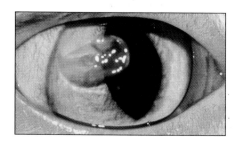

Several forms of neoplasia (cancer) can affect the conjunctiva in cats and can be either primary tumours arising in the conjunctiva or secondary, spreading from elsewhere in the body.

SCLERA

The sclera is the white fibrous coat of the globe. It is partially covered by conjunctiva and protects the more fragile internal structures. Congenital defects of this structure are very rare. Inflammation (scleritis and episcleritis) is a problem in dogs and humans but is extremely rare in cats. Feline

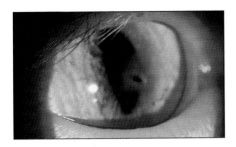

scleral diseases are usually associated with trauma and cancer.

Pre-Corneal Tear Film

This forms from tears and moistens, lubricates and helps protect the cornea. Decreased tear production occurs if the tear glands are not working properly and results in a condition called 'dry eye' or keratoconjunctivis sicca (KCS). The cornea becomes dry and roughened, leading to keratitis and ulceration. It can occur following feline herpesvirus (FHV) infection, trauma, facial paralysis and chronic inflammation.

Overproduction of tears can be seen as a result of ocular pain. The naso-lacrimal duct drains the tears; it runs from the inner corner of the eye to just inside the end of the nose. Congenital defects, such as a small duct opening, result in tear overflow and staining around the eye. These can usually be corrected surgically. Acquired blockages may result from chronic conjunctivitis or foreign bodies.

Tear staining is also seen in short-nosed breeds because the duct is tortuous and drainage inadequate. This is also associated with medial lower lid entropion, occluding the duct opening. This anatomical combination is very difficult to improve surgically.

Corneal foreign body.

Cornea

The cornea is the clear circular area at the front of the eye through which the iris and pupil can be seen. Light passes through and is focused by the cornea, before passing through the lens and hence onto the retina. Congenital defects are rare but include micro- and megalocornea. There is sometimes a transient cloudiness following the kitten's opening of the eyes but it should disappear by four weeks of age.

One of the most common problems involving the cornea is ulceration, where the top layer of corneal cells (the epithelium) is lost and the nerve endings exposed, resulting in ocular pain. Fluorescein is a special stain that can be used to reveal ulcers; they show up as a yellow/green patch on the cornea. If your cat has had this performed, you may have

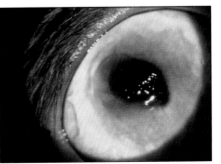

Corneal sequestrum.

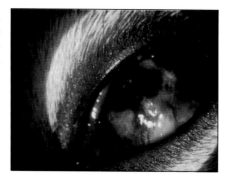

noticed the stain appearing at the end of its nose; this is because it drains down the naso-lacrimal duct and demonstrates that it is not blocked.

The most common cause of ulceration is trauma, from fight wounds or foreign bodies. FHV can cause ulceration. There is also a form of ulceration where the epithelium does not stick down again after healing and can easily become detached. This is seen as a breed-related problem in dogs. In cats, it can be seen in older animals or associated with FHV infection, resulting in recurrent ulcer formation.

The cornea is very quick to repair ulcers and, provided that the initial cause is removed, healing should only take a few days. Antibiotics are often applied to the eye while ulcers heal to prevent bacterial infection. Ulcers need prompt veterinary attention as they can deteriorate rapidly; deep ulcers can lead to rupture of the eye and require urgent surgical repair.

The cornea is a common site for cat scratch injuries and some may even penetrate the full thickness into the anterior chamber. If these wounds are repaired quickly and appropriate medical therapy is used, vision can usually be preserved. More severe ones may require reconstructive surgery, removal of the lens or even surgical removal of the eye.

Corneal foreign bodies usually result in ocular pain and need to be removed. Non-painful ones also need to be removed as they may penetrate the eye, causing internal problems.

Corneal sequestrum or necrosis is a condition specific to cats. The corneal stroma (middle layer) degenerates, turns brown/black and emerges through the epithelium, causing ulceration and a foreign body reaction with signs of ocular pain. These lesions usually need to be removed surgically because of the discom-fort they cause, but a few will slough off naturally. Often a sequestrum will recur in the same eye or occur in the opposite eye at a later date. This condition is most commonly seen in Colourpoint Persians and is thought to have an inherited component. It may be related to their prominent eye position. The next most common breed with sequestra is the Burmese.

Following healing of a corneal

wound, there is usually formation of a scar, which shows up as a white mark. Unless scars are extensive, they do not usually affect vision.

FHV-RELATED EYE DISEASES

A combination of treatments is often required to treat feline herpesvirus (FHV) infection. In acute cases, kittens are often very sick and need supportive treatment and intensive nursing. Systemic and topical antibiotics are used, sometimes in combination with topical antiviral drugs. Cats that develop symblepharon after acute infection may be blinded by the condition and require new reconstructive surgical techniques. The chronic cases can be difficult to diagnose and challenging to treat. Topical antivirals can be used and in non-ulcerated cases combined with corticosteroids. More recent treatments include L-lysine (to inhibit viral replication), Cimetidine and alpha-interferon (to boost the local immune response).

The reason for chronic FHV disease is that individuals become carriers of the virus. When they are stressed, the virus is reactivated and signs of infection and the cat's immune response to it manifest in the eye. This can be a major problem in multi-cat households with carrier animals infecting kittens and adults alike.

In these cases, management changes, including the identification of carriers, use of early vaccinations and isolation of new arrivals, must be instituted.

AQUEOUS HUMOUR

The aqueous humour is a watery fluid that is responsible for maintaining pressure within the eye. If the drainage angle is blocked and aqueous cannot drain away, pressure within the eye builds up, causing glaucoma. Glaucoma due to a congenitally obstructed drainage system is an inherited problem in many breeds of dog but is rare in the cat. When glaucoma does occur in cats, it is usually acquired, with drainage blocked by inflammatory or neoplastic cells.

Anterior uveitis can result in white blood cells in the anterior chamber, which gives it a cloudy look known as aqueous flare. Infection following penetrating wounds can result in pus accumulating in the chamber, known as hypopyon. Trauma to the eye and intra-ocular tumours may lead to bleeding into the anterior chamber

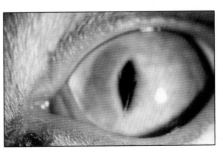

Herpesvirus ulcer.

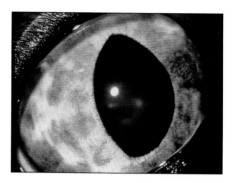

(space behind the cornea and in front of the iris), known as hyphaema. This blood usually forms a clot and is absorbed. Foreign bodies can also occasionally be seen in the anterior chamber.

IRIS AND CILIARY BODY

The iris and ciliary body are muscular and vascular structures that lie behind the cornea and in front of the lens. The iris is pigmented and gives the cat's eye its colour. Congenital defects are rare but occasionally cats are born with pieces of the iris missing. Changes in iris colour can occur for a number of reasons; as young cats mature, their iris colour may deepen. Inflammation results in reddening of the iris, due to an increase in blood vessels' formation and engorgement, and is known as rubeosis iridis. Following inflammation, the iris can remain permanently dark. As cats age, they can develop a condition called melanosis. This is usually, but not always, a diffuse change, occurring slowly in both eyes. It must be

monitored and differentiated from iris melanoma. Melanoma is a tumour of the pigment cells that can result in either diffuse or nodular discoloration of the iris. It usually progresses quickly and only in one eye. This type of neoplasia has a potential to spread outside the eye and is usually treated by surgically removing the affected eye.

A difference in colour between the two irises is known as heterochromia iridis and can occur naturally in white or poorly pigmented breeds, usually associated with congenital deafness. In other cats, it usually indicates a problem in one eye or the other.

The ciliary body and iris are known as the anterior uvea, while the choroid (the vascular layer that lies between the retina and the sclera and provides a blood supply to the retina) is the posterior uvea. Uveitis is an inflammation of the uvea. It may involve both the anterior and posterior uvea and has many causes in the cat. The main infectious causes are feline

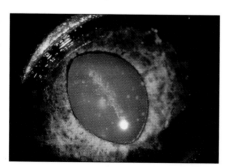

Iris melanoma, exhibited as a tumour of pigment cells that results in discoloration of the iris.

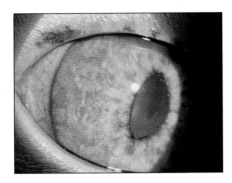

immunodeficiency virus (FIV), feline leukaemia virus (FeLV), feline infectious peritonitis (FIP) and toxoplasmosis. Tuberculosis has been reported in cats as a cause of uveitis and, in sub-tropical and tropical countries, fungal infection can be a significant cause. The signs of uveitis for all these diseases are very similar and may include a constricted pupil, rubeosis iridis, aqueous flare, poor vision and ocular pain. It can be difficult to determine the cause in some cases despite thorough investigation. Even if the primary viral infection cannot be cured, cats with uveitis can be treated symptomatically to ease discomfort and maintain vision. Long-term uveitis can lead to cataract formation, lens luxation and glaucoma. Non-infectious causes of uveitis include trauma and neoplasia.

Atrophy of the iris may occur as a result of ageing or following inflammation. Cysts of the iris are sometimes seen and look like black balloons. They form on the back of the iris but can detach and float through the pupil to rest in front. They are not neoplastic and do not usually need to be removed.

Uveitis, inflammation of the iris, ciliary body and choroid.

LENS

The lens is the clear disc-shaped structure suspended behind the iris, responsible for focusing light onto the retina. A cataract, or opacity of the lens and/or its capsule, is a disorder of the lens. Many forms of hereditary cataract are seen in dogs but not in cats. Congenital cataracts are occasionally found as a non-inherited problem. Most of the cataracts seen in cats are formed secondary to lens damage, e.g. blunt trauma, penetrating wounds, chronic anterior uveitis and lens luxation. If cataracts involve the whole lens, light will not be able to get through to the retina and the eye will be rendered blind. If appropriate, cataracts can be surgically removed.

If the lens's suspensory fibres weaken or break, it will become dislocated and can fall either into the back or front of the eye. This is a common breed-related problem in terrier dogs and is occasionally

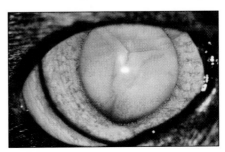

Cataract developed from long-term uveitis.

seen in cats, usually as a result of trauma, ageing or cataract. The lens is usually surgically removed to prevent it from blocking the pupil, which can lead to glaucoma.

The lens condenses with age, giving it a grey appearance, known as senile sclerosis. This is not a true cataract as light can still pass through to the back of the eye and vision is not impaired.

One rare but important condition of the lens in the cat is post-traumatic sarcoma. If the lens is damaged by trauma, it can become neoplastic and rapidly fill the eye with tumours. Appropriate treatment at the time of the initial injury should prevent this but, when it does occur, surgical removal of the eye is recommended.

VITREOUS HUMOUR

The vitreous humour is a jelly-like substance that fills the space between the back of the lens and the front of the retina. Like the aqueous humour, the vitreous can be infiltrated with haemorrhage and inflammatory cells. Foreign bodies can occasionally be found in the vitreous. Inflammation of the vitreous, known as hyalitis, can be seen as part of generalised uveitis.

The vitreous humour degenerates with age, giving a cloudy appearance to the back of the eye, but this does not usually affect vision to any great extent.

THINGS TO LOOK OUT FOR

A change in appearance of the eye
- Redness
- Cloudiness
- Change in iris colour

Increase in discharges
- Watery

Sticky mucoid
- Yellow
- Bloody

Blinking, squinting and head shyness
Aversion to light
Rubbing at the eye
Loss of vision
Protrusion of the eye
Loss of facial symmetry

RETINA

The retina, at the back of the eye, is where the visual image is formed. Congenital retinal problems are rare in cats, but colobomas (defects or holes) can occasionally be seen in the optic disc (the point at which nerves converge to leave the eye as the optic nerve). Inflammation of the retina usually occurs together with inflammation of the choroid and is called chorioretinitis or posterior uveitis. The causes are the same as those for anterior uveitis. Inflammation can lead to retinal detachment, haemorrhage, degeneration and scarring of the retina. It can be difficult to diagnose the cause of posterior uveitis; thus, symptomatic treatment is generally given to maintain vision.

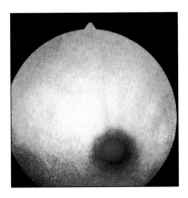

The retina may also degenerate as a result of non-inflammatory processes. An inherited form of retinal degeneration has been described in the Abyssinian and Siamese breeds. Deficiency in dietary taurine (an amino acid) causes retinal degeneration. Fortunately, this is now rare, as many commercial cat foods are supplemented with this compound. It may, however, still be a problem with some home-prepared diets.

Hypertension is a common cause of retinal disease in elderly cats. It may be primary essential hypertension or secondary to other diseases, such as kidney disease, hyperthyroidism and diabetes. Hypertension causes changes in the retinal arteries, retinal and vitreal haemorrhages, retinal detachment and hyphaema. Early recognition and treatment are essential to prevent permanent ocular damage and damage to other organs, such as the kidney, heart and brain.

Retinal detachment causes blindness and may result from hypertension, inflammation and neoplasia. If the retina does not reattach in 24–48 hours, there will be permanent vision loss. Symptomatic treatment is often given to reattach the retina, but it is also important to treat the underlying cause.

Retinal haemorrhages can occur as a result of hypertension, inflammation and trauma. They can cause temporary loss of vision but will often be resorbed. Once again, it is important to find the underlying cause and treat it accordingly without delay.

Finally, if in any doubt regarding the condition of your cat's eyes, it is always worthwhile consulting your veterinary surgeon. Even if you consider the condition minor, it may not remain so!

Advanced retinal degeneration.

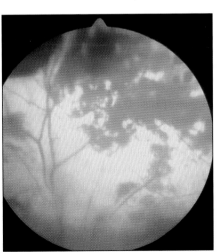

Retinal haemorrhages as a result of hypertension.

The author is grateful to the Animal Health Trust (England) for the illustrations used in the eye health section.

THE GERIATRIC CAT

Depending on lifestyle, most cats are considered old at 12 years of age. Some problems that are associated with cats in their senior years are:

• Decreased energy
• Intolerance to heat and cold
• Less meticulous grooming and litter-box habits
• Decrease in mental alertness
• Decline of liver and kidney functions
• Greater susceptibility to diseases, especially dental disease
• Increased occurrence of cancer

As long as owners pay attention and adjust for changing behaviour and diet and continue regular veterinary care, cats can live well into their teens—some even 20 years and older!

WHAT TO DO WHEN THE TIME COMES

You are never fully prepared to make a rational decision about putting your cat to sleep. It is very obvious that you love your Devon Rex or you would not be reading this book. Putting a loved cat to sleep is extremely difficult. It is a decision that must be made with your veterinary surgeon. You are usually forced to make the decision when your beloved pet will only suffer more and experience no enjoyment for the balance of its life. Then euthanasia is the right choice.

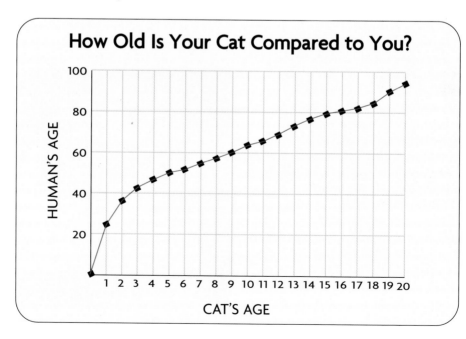

How Old Is Your Cat Compared to You?

WHAT IS EUTHANASIA?

Euthanasia derives from the Greek, meaning *good death*. In other words, it means the planned, painless killing of a cat suffering from a painful, incurable condition, or who is so aged that it cannot walk, see, eat or control its excretory functions.

Euthanasia is usually accomplished by injection with an overdose of an anaesthesia or barbiturate. Aside from the prick of the needle, the experience is usually painless.

MAKING THE DECISION

The decision to euthanise your cat is never easy. The days during which the cat becomes ill and the end occurs can be unusually stressful for you. If this is your first experience with the death of a loved one, you may need the comfort dictated by your religious beliefs. If you are the head of the family and have children, you should have involved them in the decision of putting your Devon Rex to sleep. Usually your cat can be maintained on drugs for a few days in order to give you ample time to make a decision. During this time, talking with members of your family or even people who have lived through this same experience can ease the burden of your inevitable decision.

THE FINAL RESTING PLACE

Cats can have some of the same privileges as humans. The remains of your beloved cat can be buried in a pet cemetery, which is generally expensive. Cats who have died at home can be buried in your garden in a place suitably marked with some stone or newly planted tree or bush. Alternatively, they can be cremated individually and the ashes returned to you. A less expensive option is mass cremation, although, of course, the ashes can not then be returned. Vets can usually arrange the cremation on your behalf. The cost of these options should always be discussed frankly and openly with your veterinary surgeon.

The remains of your beloved Devon Rex can be buried in a pet cemetery.

USEFUL ADDRESSES

GREAT BRITAIN
The Governing Council of the Cat Fancy (GCCF)
4-6 Penel Orlieu, Bridgwater, Somerset, TA6 3PG
Email: GCCF_CATS@compuserve.com Fax: 01278 446627 Tel: 01278 427575

The Cat Association of Britain
Mill House, Letcombe Regis, Oxon OX12 9JD   Tel: 01235 766543

EUROPE
Federation Internationale Feline (FIFe)
Gen. Sec: Ms Penelope Bydlinski.
Little Dene, Lenham Heath, Maidstone, Kent ME17 2BS, GB
Email: penbyd@compuserve.com   Fax: 1622 850193 Tel: 1622 850908

World Cat Federation
Hubertsrabe 280, D-45307, Essen, Germany
Email: wcf@nrw-online.de   Fax: 201-552747 Tel: 201-555724

AUSTRALIA
The Australian Cat Federation, Inc.
PO Box 3305, Port Adelaide, SA 5015
Email: acf@catlover.com   Fax: 08 8242 2767 Tel: 08 8449 5880

CANADA
Canadian Cat Association
220 Advance Boulevard, Suite 101, Brampton, Ontario L6T 4J5
Email: office@cca-afc.com   Fax: 99050 459-4023 Tel: 99060 4591481

SOUTH AFRICA
Cat Federation of Southern Africa
PO Box 25, Bromhof 2154, Gauteng Province, Republic of South Africa

USA
American Cat Association
8101 Katherine Avenue, Panorama City, CA 91402
Fax: (818) 781-5340 Tel: (818) 781-5656

American Cat Fanciers Association
PO Box 203, Point Lookout, MO 65726
Email: info@acfacat.com   Fax: (417) 334-5540 Tel: (417) 334-5430

Cat Fanciers Association, Inc. (CFA)
PO Box 1005, Manasquan, NJ 08736-0805
Email: cfa@cfainc.org   Fax: (732) 528-7391 Tel: (732) 528-9797

Cat Fanciers Federation
PO Box 661, Gratis, OH 45330
Email: Lalbert933@aol.com Fax: (937) 787-4290 Tel: (937) 787-9009

The International Cat Association
PO Box 2684, Harlingen, TX 78551
Email: ticaeo@xanadu2.net Tel: (956) 428-8046